Praise for *Picking Up the Pieces*

"| ol
th: ject
     ,
     "

"Being a victim of crime can be devastating, overwhelming, and physically and emotionally draining. Addiction adds another layer to an already difficult process. Jennifer Storm understands and has thrived and survived both sides of the coin. She has found a simplistic, straightforward way to share invaluable insight into the many facets of a victim's journey through uncharted waters. Throughout *Picking Up the Pieces,* she is gentle and honest as she provides guidance on the emotional roller coaster a victim is forced to ride, validating the good and not-so-good feelings, how to navigate the criminal justice system, and so much more. Thousands will benefit from Jen's work."

Lynn Shiner
Homicide survivor
Director, Office of Victims' Services, Pennsylvania Commission on Crime and Delinquency

* * *

"*Picking Up the Pieces* is a wonderful guide to understanding your emotions at each level of your recovery. Jennifer's genuine insight will help many who need it."

Mildred D Muhammad
Author of *Scared Silent: When the One You Love...Becomes the One You Fear*
Founder/Executive Director of After the Trauma, Inc.

* * *

"A guidebook that I would highly recommend to any victim as he or she struggles to find a 'new normal.' Jennifer Storm has compassionately composed exercises that empower one to transition from darkness into light. Each chapter is written from Jennifer's first-hand experiences with the anger, guilt, and shame of her own personal struggle to survive. The author's devotion to her work is evident by her passion to assist others to follow her path from pain to recovery."

Debra Puglisi Sharp
Author of *Shattered: Reclaiming a Life Torn Apart by Violence*

Picking

Up

the

Pieces

without

Picking

Up

Picking Up the Pieces WITHOUT Picking Up

A GUIDEBOOK THROUGH VICTIMIZATION FOR PEOPLE IN RECOVERY

by Jennifer Storm

CENTRAL RECOVERY PRESS

Central Recovery Press (CRP) is committed to publishing exceptional materials addressing addiction treatment, recovery, and behavioral health care topics, including original and quality books, audio/visual communications, and web-based new media. Through a diverse selection of titles, we seek to contribute a broad range of unique resources for professionals, recovering individuals and their families, and the general public.

For more information, visit www.centralrecoverypress.com.
Central Recovery Press, Las Vegas, NV 89129
©2011 by Jennifer Storm
ISBN-13: 978-1-936290-64-2 (paper)
ISBN-10: 1-936290-64-2

17 16 15 14 13 12 11   1 2 3 4 5
Publisher: Central Recovery Press
             3321 N. Buffalo Drive
             Las Vegas, NV 89129

EDITOR'S NOTE: Our books represent the experiences and opinions of their authors only. Every effort has been made to ensure that events, institutions, and statistics presented in our books as facts are accurate and up-to-date.

Cover design and interior by Sara Streifel, Think Creative Design

*This book is dedicated to Margaret Colby, my sister,
my best friend, my soul mate, and my sponsor of twelve years.
Your constant and daily love is something I miss more than
words on this paper can ever convey. There is an empty space
in my heart that your voice and laughter used to fill.
Without your influence in my life, this book would have
never come to be—nor would I be who I am today.
Thank you for everything, until we meet again.*

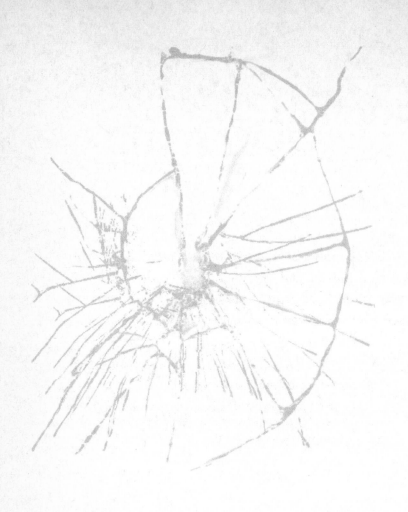

Table of Contents

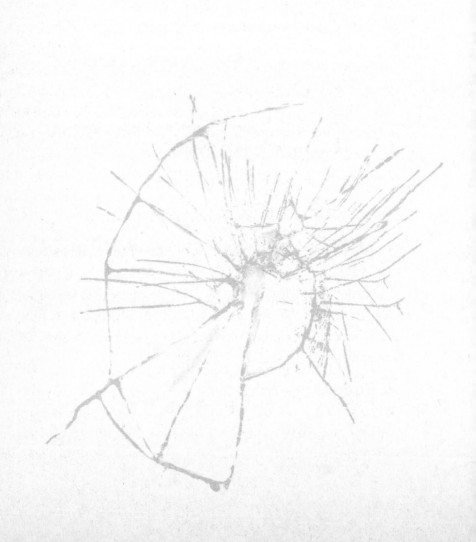

Preface

I am a crime victim/survivor a few times over. When I was twelve I was a raped by a man who was twenty-eight years old. That night was the first time I ever had a drink in my life, and I was hooked the minute the fluid hit my lips. I wound up blacking out, and a night of innocent roller skating turned into the single worst night of my life. The crime and its aftermath took my life and twisted it into something I didn't recognize. When I looked in the mirror I no longer knew the reflection looking back. Everything I knew had been shattered, and there were pieces of my former life all over the floor around me and my family. My brother, my parents, and I walked carefully among these shards, fearful that we might find a sharp edge and cut ourselves deeper than we had already been injured. Our home became a live land mine, and none of us knew how to walk around normally anymore.

I had no methods, resources, or understanding of how to begin to heal. I was so lost, and the fact that alcohol was involved in my victimization only fueled the guilt train I jumped on immediately. Instead of turning away from alcohol, I ran toward it. It became the solution to my problems, not the source. I didn't ease into addiction like some do over years and years of social use—I slammed into it.

My active addiction went on into my teenage years and early twenties. Of course, living a lifestyle of drinking until blackout or running the streets in the middle of the night to purchase illegal drugs led me straight into additional victimization. For many years I had a hard time deciphering what was truly my role in the victimization. It wasn't until I found recovery by going to a rehabilitation center that I realized that no one had the right to harm me, regardless of what I was doing. My addiction and victimization were so intertwined that it took me a long time in recovery to untwist all my false understandings and come to a place of peace and forgiveness with it all.

I wound up going to college to become a drug and alcohol counselor. I wanted to give back what I had found, which was a way of life I never knew was possible. It was a life free from addiction and full of possibility. As I progressed in college I began to learn about victims' rights, a concept that was foreign to me. I never knew crime victims had rights. Even as a victim, I had never had anyone educate me on these things. I learned that in the early 1980s a movement brought about a bill of rights for crime victims, and that each state in the nation had its own version of these rights.

I was intrigued, and upon graduation I sought a position working to create change for crime victims in my state. I lobbied for legislation and did a lot of educational planning in my first job as managing director of a statewide coalition. I was then hired as the executive director of a nonprofit organization that provides direct services to crime victims in Dauphin County, Harrisburg, Pennsylvania. The Victim/ Witness Assistance Program provides services to more than eight thousand victims each year, and I am in my eighth year working with this amazing program. It was in my work with this agency that I began to discover how much victims' services had to offer. In my first year I responded to more than twenty homicides; provided death notification, crisis intervention, and supportive counseling; assisted with body identification and transfer; and linked families and loved ones to victims' compensation. I've worked with victims of theft, rape, domestic violence, homicide, assault, and other crimes.

I wanted to write this book not only from the viewpoint of a survivor of crime, but as a person in recovery and as an executive director of a program that works directly with crime victims. So often when my agency is working with clients, we discover that substance abuse or addiction is an underlying factor—whether the client is struggling or the offender was addicted at the time of the crime. I wanted to create an easy-to-follow guide that would allow people to understand not only the trauma they are experiencing, but also how the criminal justice system works and is expected to treat them. Additionally, I felt a strong need to address the co-occurring substance abuse issues.

When attempting to heal from victimization, it is easy to fall back into old patterns of addiction, or, if you've never experienced problems with alcohol and other drugs, to now find yourself using substances to cope. This book is intended to serve as an educational resource that will walk you through your pain, help you navigate the criminal justice system, and give you helpful guidance on dealing and healing. As a survivor myself, I wish a resource like this had been available when I needed it. I am humbled to be in a position to provide this guide to you, and I hope it helps you as we all trudge along this journey together in one way or another. May peace be with you.

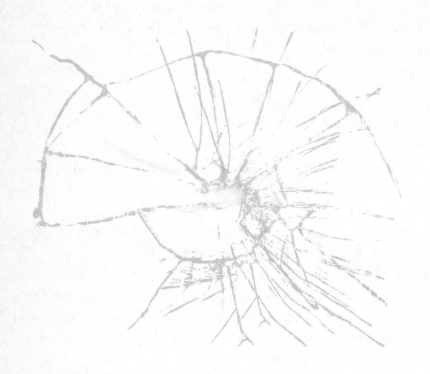

Acknowledgments

I want to express sincere gratitude to the staff at Central Recovery Press for believing in me and my writing; in no specific order, their fabulousness is made up of Nancy Schenck, Patrick Hughes, Valerie Killeen, Bob Gray, Helen O'Reilly, and Dan Mager. To Thomas Woll and Kae Tienstra for working so hard to promote my work.

Thank you for believing in my work and making it better. Thank you to my agent, Devra Ann Jacobs, and my manager, Phyllis Parsons—two amazing and tireless women.

As always, to my amazing, supportive, and loving family, James and Pat Storm, James Storm, Jr., Brian Storm, and my two awesome nieces, Cheyanne Storm and Amelia Storm.

Fianne Van Schaaik, for your unconditional love, your honest critique of my writing, and your unwavering support. You have believed in me at times when I haven't believed in myself. You are forever my cheerleader; thank you so much for that.

My staff of amazing advocates who in many ways have inspired so much of what you see on the pages of this book. The dedication and hard work you bring to the job every day are beyond admirable. You are my family and I love you all.

Last, but never least, to each and every person out there who has been victimized in some way, you are never alone. There is a way to heal, and your life can be amazing again—I promise.

Introduction

Today you are on a new path, one that you wouldn't and couldn't have chosen, one that is unfamiliar and scary, and one that undoubtedly you would give anything to venture away from. There will be questions at every turn you encounter. Your balance is off, and the once-stable surface beneath your feet suddenly feels like it is caving in. You feel yourself sinking, shifting, changing. You open your eyes hoping it was all a dream, only to be smacked with the reality of daylight and the brutal realization that it wasn't. Nothing looks the same through your eyes anymore, as though someone put a pair of glasses on you that you cannot take off, and you can only see the same horrible show over and over again. You are a victim or you are a witness to victimization.

Everything you previously knew and felt and thought fades into the background as the victimization stands out as the only reality. Your life today operates as only two segments: before the crime and after the crime. There no longer is a gray period, only black and white, before and after.

Just when you thought recovery couldn't get any harder, life on life's terms happens, and sometimes that means someone perpetrating violence upon you or your home. One of our most fundamental rights as citizens is to live in peace without the threat of violence and crime. Unfortunately, at times our rights may be compromised. Too many of us have been victims of a violent crime, or know a family member or friend who has been.

If you're reading this book, then either you or a loved one has been the victim of a crime and you are seeking help. Make no mistake about it; even if your loved one is the victim, you too become a victim of sorts. You see, feel, and hear the pain the primary victim goes through, and it is impossible for it not to permeate your soul and leave an imprint on you that can be just as confusing as the crime itself. Although the crime wasn't perpetrated against you, you nonetheless find yourself with similar emotions as the victim's in the aftermath. Being the victim or a witness of a crime can be the single most traumatic event a person experiences in his or her lifetime. My hope is that this book will serve as a guide to help you along your healing journey.

All too often victimization occurs while a person is engaging in addictive behavior, whether it is with alcohol or other drugs, sex, or some other manifestation of the disease of addiction. This only adds to the guilt, shame, and horror you may feel about the crime and your actions surrounding the crime. Additionally, people who are already in recovery from addiction may find their recovery in jeopardy as a result of being victimized and the increased stress and emotional distress that come along with it. This book will guide you through these emotions while educating you on the criminal justice system and on ways to safeguard your recovery—or find recovery.

Whether your victimization was due to the murder of a loved one, rape, sexual assault, burglary, identity theft, child abuse, domestic violence, aggravated assault, or another type of crime, you are left with the feeling that nothing feels as it once did, and it may never again.

There are three things I want you to know:

1. You are not alone.

2. You will get through this.

3. Picking up a drink or other substance will only make this worse.

The next hours, days, and months are going to be difficult, but not impossible, to get through. Your emotions will swing, sometimes wildly, from one extreme to another as you find a way to come to terms with what has happened to you. This book is here to help during this most difficult time, to empathize with you, and to ultimately help you heal. It cannot take away what happened to you, it cannot replace the loss you feel, and it will not attempt to tell you how to feel or grieve. What it can offer you is guidance that will assist you in navigating this uncharted territory—guidance from a person who has been through a similar journey and who has guided hundreds through their own journeys.

In this book you will find many useful tools to help you along this new path, including critical information about the criminal justice system and victims' rights that you will need in the weeks and months ahead of you, valuable insight about the stages of grief and how to cope with the feelings and emotions you may be experiencing, and recovery-oriented exercises that you will be able to carry with you to ensure your recovery isn't jeopardized by the trauma you are facing.

Consider this guidebook your new best friend—you can pick it up at any point and turn a page to find activities, resources, affirmations, and reminders that you need to get through the day. Again, you are not alone; information and support are but a page away. The beauty of this book is that you do not have to read it from beginning to end. You can pick it up and go straight to the chapter you need at any given time. If your criminal case is moving through the justice system, it will be especially helpful to read Chapters Eight and Nine to help inform and prepare you for that process. You can also read this book cover to cover if you wish. However you choose to embrace this journey is up to you. You might pick this book up and put it down a hundred times, and that is okay. This is all in your time, and all I ask is that you attempt each exercise with an open mind about processing your feelings.

I advise you to purchase a separate notebook or journal for making notes, answering questions, and completing the exercises and activities provided. Each chapter will end with an exercise that is relevant to what was discussed in the chapter, to provide you with a deeper and more meaningful way to connect the information to your specific situation. Additionally, you will find that at the beginning of each chapter I ask that you make a gratitude list. As the chapters progress, the number of items I ask you to identify that you are grateful for increases. I have found that in my recovery, whenever I am struggling, looking for purpose, feeling down, feeling less than, and so on, nothing lifts me up and brings me back into balance more effectively than making a quick gratitude list. In times of struggle it can be so easy to focus on all that is wrong around us and to not see the good that still exists. By taking the time before each chapter to make a gratitude list, you will be able to see, each time, one more thing you do have in your life that you can be grateful for. The new item on your list could simply be a piece of information or insight you learned from the previous chapter; it could be that the sun is shining; it could be that your cat or dog just curled up in your lap and gave you affection; it could be that you found the courage to open this book today. Whatever it is, I want you to identify it and begin each chapter with some gratitude and positivity.

I do hope this book enables you to process your feelings and bring yourself back into harmony with your recovery, and that it empowers you to truly believe that you can overcome the unthinkable just by putting one foot in front of the other. By getting this far, you are already on your way toward doing just that.

Take a moment to write here or on a separate piece
of paper, or just process out loud or in your mind,
a gratitude list.

What is something you are grateful for today?

_____

_____

_____

_____

_____

_____

_____

_____

_____

_____

_____

_____

_____

_____

CHAPTER ONE

When Crime Hits Home

You have just found yourself a part of a statistic you no doubt never wished to be included in—a crime victim. You are not alone. Crime affects more than a million households each and every year, leaving many people in its wake with more questions than answers. You are in shock; you feel numb, confused, and in disbelief. Emotions like anger, fear, despair, confusion, hatred, denial, indifference, and many more are also common. You may not be able to even identify your emotions right now, as they may all be swirling around you and closing in on you at every turn.

Right now, I want you to stop, take a deep breath, and exhale. Repeat this ten times. Clear your mind and try to regain your footing while you begin to take the first critical steps toward healing. Although it may feel like no one else in the world could relate to what you are going through right now, I promise you that is not the case. If you cannot even put into words what you are feeling, know that that is normal. You are taking a positive step by opening this book and trying to sort through the wreckage that has become your life. Today is a good day because you are doing something good for yourself. I want you to acknowledge this to yourself.

AFFIRMATION

Today I am doing okay. I survived, and I am alive. I do not have to let this crime define me. I am a good person, and I did absolutely nothing to bring this act of violence into my life. It's not my fault. I am not responsible for the actions of others.

The fact that you are reading this book is a step toward your healing. Even if you just open it and close it, you have done something positive. Remember, there is no timeline for completing this book. While it will be your guide through the criminal justice process, you do not have to follow each and every section or task at the same time you are experiencing the events surrounding your case. This is your journey, and you are in control of how you progress through it. This book is here to serve as a tool to help you identify your emotions and process them in a healthy way, and to educate and empower you about the criminal justice system you now involuntarily find yourself participating in.

I am so sorry this has happened to you. I am sorry that a person or people have come into your life and shifted your reality. I am sorry you have been harmed both emotionally and physically. You did not deserve this. You did not invite this crime into your life. We all have the right to live in this world with the promise of security and safety. I am sorry someone has taken your security. I know it feels like the foundation you once walked upon is now shaky and uncertain, and some days just to get up out of bed and take one step takes all the effort you can muster. If you managed to do that today, then I say congratulations to you. That is indeed an important first step. I cannot promise you that you will ever feel 100 percent safe again. The healing process will take time. For some, it will take only a few months or years to regain their footing. For others, it will be a longer journey. Always keep in mind that it is a journey—there is no end point in personal growth and recovery.

We all walk each and every day with the understanding that we only have today. We do not have to do everything perfectly today, as that is impossible to do. But we need to participate in the process, and sometimes we just need to suit up and show up. If you are reading this chapter today, then you have done that, and that is something to be proud of.

In recovery we often hear "one day at a time," but when trauma and victimization come into our lives it often feels like we can only make it one hour at a time, or even one minute at a time. That is also true of early recovery—it can be a minute-by-minute struggle, and this is no different. If you can make it through the next couple of minutes that it takes to get to the end of this page, then you have done something important for yourself.

Your life has changed. Everything is different today. Everyone you once trusted has become suspect. Every certainty about the world and your existence in it is being challenged. But here is what you do know today: you are alive, you are in recovery, and you are not alone.

> There is nothing in your life today
> that a drink or drug or your
> addictive behavior of choice won't
> make ten times worse.

Be gentle with yourself. Just as your journey in recovery from addiction holds no timeline but your own, the same applies for your healing from this trauma. No one can speed up this process for you, and no one has the right to dictate your course of action. It probably feels like there is no one around who can understand or relate to your pain. In some ways you are correct—your feelings and emotions associated with this experience are unique to you. But the important thing to know is that you don't need to feel alone. While others may not be able to fully understand the depth of your grief or pain, there are many people around you who are willing to be there for you to lend a listening ear, a shoulder to cry on, arms to surround you with a hug, and a smile to give you hope. Find these people in your life.

They will become your greatest assets in the upcoming days, months, and years. They may come in unlikely forms. You may feel there is no one in your family or group of friends who can offer this, and if that is the case, look outside your immediate support system. There are victim advocates in your community who are willing and able to provide this assistance to you. If no one has reached out to you already, please find someone. Almost every town, county, or city has victim advocates or coordinators. Check your local phone directory, search online, or call your local police department to find out where they are. Chapter Eight will go into detail about what a victim advocate is and what he or she can offer you during your time in the criminal justice system. It is crucial that you have people you can call.

Right now your entire life lens has been shattered. Think of yourself before the crime. You had a clear vision of what your life looked like, and you were comfortable with that vision. Since the crime occurred it may feel like someone took your glasses off, shattered the lenses, and then put them back on your face. Now your vision is blurry and distorted, and nothing looks the same around you. This is a very normal response to a very abnormal event that has occurred in your life. Your world and your view of it have been altered. It will take time to pick up those pieces and put them back together. Your vision may be blurry for a while, but at some point, I can promise you, you will see clearly again. You will recognize the world again. It will just take time, and it will be a different world and a different view.

To do this you will need tools. Just as with the rebuilding of anything, be it a house, a car, or a community, you need the right tools to get the job done.

EXERCISE

Think about what it is you need to begin to heal. In order to know what you need, it is important to first identify how you feel. Try to identify what you are feeling right now. It is okay if you do not know exactly how you feel; just begin by writing whatever comes up for you in this moment. Use a separate journal or notebook, or if you do not have one, grab a piece of paper and begin writing.

Close your eyes and take ten long, deep breaths. Try to quiet your mind as you focus solely on your breathing—breathing in deeply through the nose, filling your lungs to capacity, and then blowing all that stale air out through your mouth and into the universe. Once you have completed ten of these, try to articulate on paper your answers to these questions:

1. What would help you right now?

2. What is the one thing you could use that would make you feel better?

3. What would help you sleep, breathe easier, smile?

It is okay if you left some questions blank or if your answers are filled with negative thoughts, such as "I could use a drink." I want you to be as honest as you possibly can in these exercises. It is natural for those of us in recovery to want to engage in addictive behaviors when bad things happen. Heck, it was normal for us to want to engage in our addictive behaviors when good things happened, so why wouldn't we look to those things we once used in order to help us through something terrible? As addicts, this is part of our reality and our process. However, today we do not have to give in to the negative thoughts and the old behaviors that led us to pain, remorse, and destruction in our lives. Today we have a choice. In our active addiction it was our knee-jerk reaction to reach for something outside of ourselves to help us deal with what was going on inside of us. Usually those things were not beneficial to our recovery or our lives.

> Recovery is a learned set of behaviors, and like any behavior or habit, we must practice it in order to keep it functioning properly.

Think of your recovery as a muscle; you need to flex it often to keep it in shape. The great thing about muscles is that they have amazing memory, so if you haven't flexed your muscle in a while, that is okay, because as soon as you do it will remember and work with you quickly.

Our secrets will keep us sick. We must expose our deepest and darkest thoughts and feelings or they will harm us. This is your safe space to do that. Let it out. Use your journal now to expose those thoughts. The very act of taking them from inside of you and putting them out in writing in front of you is an extremely brave and powerful act. If you cannot list them all now, you can leave blank spaces to fill in at a later time if you need to.

Building your support system

"When I received the news that my son had been murdered, I immediately thought of a drink. I just wanted to numb the pain. Thankfully, I had a support system around me to remind me that a drink would only make it worse."

You cannot do this alone. No one can. It is vital for you to begin to build a support system around you during this time. You will need people to call and talk to for emotional support. You will also need guidance as you walk through the criminal justice system. Victim advocates and victim assistance coordinators are available to walk you through this process.

EXERCISE

Think of the people in your life who you can call right now for help. These can include a pastor, a friend, a family member, a teacher, a police officer, an advocate—anyone you feel comfortable talking to. Take a moment now to make a list of those you already know you can call. List their names, relationships to you, and ways to contact them, such as email addresses and phone numbers. Additionally, list exactly what each person can offer you. Can he or she provide facts, emotional support, a solid listening ear, good advice?

The following table contains suggestions for you to consider when building your support system. You may have already listed some of these, and if so, great—you are beginning to understand what it takes to start healing. If you didn't have these listed, that is okay too. You cannot be expected to know what you need or want right now. Remember to be gentle with yourself.

Emotional support	Someone who can hug you, listen to you, and give you a shoulder to cry on. Someone you can call at any hour of the night or day and who will be there to offer support.
Guidance support	Someone who has information and resources that will be helpful to you, such as a victim advocate, a counselor, a police officer or coordinator in the police department, or your sponsor.
Distraction support	Someone you can go and have fun with, who will help take your mind off everything and allow you to just be you.
Recovery support	Someone who can get you to a meeting or a support group that can help you with your specific situation.

- Try to identify a handful of people who you know today can offer this support to you.

- Have you had contact with your sponsor or counselor? If you do not have a sponsor in a recovery program, do you have a support system or an advocate you can call and check in with on a daily basis?

You are going to find that you need a range of assistance. Sometimes you will need a person to listen to you, other times you will need to cry and you will need a hug, and sometimes you will need information. The following exercise is to help you sort through and list your contacts so will you have a quick reference guide when you need it. These people will make up your core support system. You may have one or two names or you may have ten, as long as you have at least one.

People I can call for help (based on the four types of support)

SUPPORT TYPE:	Emotional	Guidance	Distraction	Recovery
Name				
Relationship				
Contact info				
What can this person offer				

EMOTIONAL SUPPORT

Whom can I call when I need a hug or a shoulder to cry on?

Whom can I call when I need to vent and just need someone to listen?

Whom can I call in the middle of the night?

GUIDANCE SUPPORT

Who is the police officer working on my case?

Who is my victim advocate?

Where can I go for counseling or a support group?

DISTRACTION SUPPORT

With whom can I do some physical activity (for instance, running, walking)?

With whom can I do something fun (for instance, a movie, games)?

RECOVERY SUPPORT

Whom can I call to give me a ride to meetings so I don't have to go alone?

Whom can I ask to keep me accountable with my recovery meetings and to ensure I am getting to them?

Where can I find a support group of others who have experienced similar situations?

You may not have a vast support system, and that is okay; you can begin to build one. Try to think of what is missing in the support group you listed, and identify where you can find that support.

EXERCISE

Are there any other types of support that you need at this time? If yes, what are they?

Acknowledging what you are powerless over

Jane's house was broken into last winter; almost everything she and her family valued was stolen while they were out one night. She had to remind herself each day that she was powerless over the things she had lost. She could not will them back; she could not change the fact that her family felt scared each night; she could not control that she woke up at exactly 2:30 each morning in a panic.

Treat your healing from this crime just like you did in your early recovery. It will take baby steps, and these steps must be taken in your time and within your comfort level. Just like in early recovery when we had to acknowledge that we were powerless over our addiction, we must also accept that we are powerless over the crime that has affected us. We cannot change what has happened to us. The only thing in our control is how we move forward. The crime that permeated your life has rocked your control center. It may feel like your life is out of control right now, but it's not—not totally. Determining for yourself what is in your control and what is simply beyond your reach will help you understand what next steps you can take and should take to move toward your healing. I'd like to help you to identify the things you are powerless over right now.

EXERCISE

Complete this statement: I am powerless over _____.

Just as we do in the First Step of the Twelve Steps of recovery, we must determine what in our life is now unmanageable as a result of the crime that has infiltrated our way of life. By making a list of ways our life is now unmanageable, we can determine how to bring those things back into a manageable place. Awareness is the key. If we know what we need and what we lack, we can help bring our lives back into a harmonious balance. Take a moment now to list ways your life is currently unmanageable.

Admitting we are powerless and that an area of our lives has become unmanageable can be a humbling experience. After all, we are responsible adults; we have tackled recovery, and now we are faced once again with feeling like we are starting over emotionally. We may have been taught that to be in control means we are successful. Relinquishing that control can be such a challenge. Victimization and trauma temporarily remove control from our lives, as the act of another has swept in and caused a shift in our balance. In what ways do you feel stressed or overwhelmed by the lack of balance in your life today?

Applying Step One to your healing process

To admit we are powerless over a situation, person, or thing is an extreme act of humility that requires us to override our egos and accept that there isn't anything we can do. However, there are extraordinary gifts in the First Step and in this act of admission and submission. Truly understanding that we are completely powerless over something that has happened to us can ease the heavy burden of guilt that many crime victims carry around. You were powerless; you couldn't have changed the outcome of this crime regardless of what you did or didn't do. For some, Step One can offer some relief as it respectfully shifts responsibility to the party who should be held responsible—the offender.

This does not mean that you remain powerless; you have the power to take the necessary steps toward healing and regaining that vital balance we all strive for in recovery and life. Balance is the full understanding that while life may shift from one extreme to the next, we have the ability to pull ourselves—physically, mentally, emotionally, and spiritually—back into the center. The center is that place where we are neither hysterical nor apathetic; rather, it is a place of soft and calm where we can see ourselves in our truest form. We can think clearly and react to anything that comes our way in an authentic and honorable way. We can behave in a manner that is consistent with who we truly are, and not in a reactionary, emotionally extreme, or emotionally absent way.

In so many ways this level of balance is the crux of a solid recovery program. I know for me personally, my life is all about finding the balance and maintaining it always. I am at my best when I feel balanced. Stress, victimization, and crime shake our balance like nothing else, and the best way to get that balance back lies within our degree of self-awareness and our ability to have an understanding of ourselves.

EXERCISE

In our active addiction, it's all about extremes and swinging from one extreme to the next. Recovery and healing are about pulling those extremes into balance. The same can be said for recovering from a trauma in our lives. In order to do that, we must understand what we can change and what we cannot. So think about what is within your reach and what you do have control over today. What can you change today?

Today I have the ability to control . . . (For instance, I can get out of bed, take a shower, make a to-do list.)

Congratulations on completing this first chapter. You are off to a great start. You now have a list of people and tools you can turn to when you need them. During those times when you need emotional support, guidance support, distraction support, or meeting support, you now know exactly whom to call. You have also identified some of your initial feelings and needs. You have realized once again in your life that you are not in control and could be way out of balance. Let's end this chapter with the axis of recovery, the Serenity Prayer.

God, grant me the serenity
To accept the things I cannot change,
Courage to change the things I can,
And wisdom to know the difference.

Take a moment to write here or on a separate piece
of paper, or just process out loud or in your mind,
a gratitude list.

What are two things you are grateful for today?

_____

_____

_____

_____

_____

_____

_____

_____

_____

_____

_____

_____

_____

_____

_____

_____

CHAPTER TWO

Reactions to Crisis and Trauma

*"I didn't respond the way I thought I would.
What is wrong with me?"*

*"How could I have just stood there
and let this happen?"*

**Whether you screamed, fought back, froze in your tracks, or figured
out a way to adapt to what was happening to you, your reaction
was the right reaction for you given the extreme circumstances.
How you thought you would respond to a traumatic event isn't
always the way your body and mind choose to cope.** We are all
prewired to respond a certain way to a crisis situation, and it isn't
always the way we think we would respond. There are chemical and
medical explanations for what your mind, body, and spirit went through.
This chapter will help you to understand the effects a crisis and trauma
have on your brain and emotional well-being. Understanding why you
are feeling the way you are and that there are chemical and medical
reasons for your reaction to this crisis will help in your recovery.

Just as we are powerless in our addiction over our chemical, physical, and psychological response to a drug once it hits our system, we are sometimes powerless over our responses to extreme stress and trauma.

"I didn't understand my reaction to the rape. I felt like I should have responded differently; I should have screamed or fought—but I didn't. I beat myself up over this for years until I learned about crisis response and realized my reaction was quite normal and out of my control."

First and foremost, if you are beating yourself up for responding the way you did, stop. Your response was just as much out of your control as the crime itself. You could never have predicted exactly how you would respond, so please do not waste any of your energy or time beating yourself up for not responding the way you thought you would have or should have. Playing the "would've" and "should've" game will only serve to make you crazy.

AFFIRMATION

Today I will stop beating myself up for the way I responded to the crime. My response during this crime was not right or wrong; it was simply beyond my control. However, today I have control over how I will respond to my feelings about this event.

How trauma throws off physical and emotional balance

Most people go through each day in a normal state of equilibrium or balance. Various stressors throughout your day can throw your equilibrium off a bit, such as a traffic jam when you're late for work, getting pulled over for a traffic violation, or realizing that you have a big project that needs to be done. These are small stressors that can create a stress response in our body; however, we have a pretty good understanding of how we will respond to these daily stressors, so we aren't totally thrown off balance when they occur. We are prepared for these types of stressors and, in many cases, we expect them. But when a significant crisis or trauma enters our world, it throws our equilibrium completely off its axis. We get so out of balance and off course that often we can't get back to our original state of being. Our lives have been altered and shifted in such a drastic way that we must understand our responses in order to understand how we will respond to additional stressors throughout our lives after the crime. Today everything has changed. In order to adapt to these changes, we must understand what has happened and why.

The following is drawn from Chapter One of Marlene A. Young's *Victim Assistance: Frontiers and Fundamentals,* a publication of the National Organization for Victim Assistance (NOVA).*

> Trauma may be brought on by either an "acute" stressor or many "chronic" stressors. In order to understand which stressor you are responding to, we must define these terms. An acute stressor is usually a sudden, arbitrary, often random event. Crimes committed by strangers are key examples of such stressors. A chronic stressor is one that occurs over and over again, each time pushing its victims toward the edge of their state of equilibrium, or beyond. Chronic child, spousal, partner, dating, or elder abuse are examples of such chronic stressors.

Used by permission of NOVA.

The crisis reaction: the physical response

Physical shock, disorientation, and numbness

Initially people often experience a state of "frozen fright" in response to a dangerous threat. They may realize that something is terribly wrong or that something bad has happened, but they cannot comprehend the event or its impact. They may be unable to move or react. They may become disoriented because seconds ago everything in their life was "normal," and now the world seems to be radically different and chaotic.

When trauma occurs, your body goes through a dramatic response physically and biologically, causing all types of responses. Adrenaline rushes through your body at lightning speed and immediately affects the body's response to the event. Once the senses detect a threat, the body generates the power to fight or flee from the situation.

"I have always thought that if someone attacked me, I would run like crazy in the other direction. But when I felt the gun pressed into my back I just froze, time stood still, and it felt like my feet were bolted to the floor beneath me. I could not move, and it really upset me. Why didn't I run?"

The reaction to fight or flee is generated by instinct and emotion. Thoughtful decision-making is rarely involved. It is impossible to predict what that first response will be. So if you have experienced a response that is counterintuitive to what you thought it would be, please be gentle with yourself. You couldn't have controlled your response if you wanted to.

"After coming home to find my home was burglarized, I began to throw up. My stomach was wretched and I couldn't breathe. I just kept thinking about what could have happened had my baby and I been in the house at the time. It made me so sick and I threw up all night long."

"I was held at gunpoint for over thirty minutes during the robbery, but it wasn't until I was giving my statement to the police that I realized my pants were soaked. I had urinated and didn't even realize it. I was so embarrassed."

Just like our emotional reaction isn't always as we would think, neither is our physical reaction. Sometimes our bodies react physically in ways we do not understand, and we may vomit, defecate, or urinate. This can be very upsetting, as it adds an additional layer of confusion and sometimes shame to the crime itself. Again, please be mindful that you cannot always control what your body will do; you were powerless over your reaction to this event. Be gentle with yourself; you are only human.

The following charts are provided by the National Organization for Victim Assistance, and help to illustrate the physical and emotional responses to crisis.

PHYSICAL

Frozen Fright
Body takes on reality of threat;
immobilization may be for a few
moments or minutes

Fight, Flight, Adaptation
Heart rate increases, blood pressure rises,
adrenaline pumps, 1 or 2 senses become
acute, body excretes toxins (regurgitation,
defecation, urination); body will fight, flee
or adapt as a survivor skill

Exhaustion
Yesterday—Today—Tomorrow
Past—Present—Future
Body exhausts itself to relax so it can make
more adrenaline; often equated with
sleeping, though most victims don't sleep

EMOTIONAL

Shock, Disbelief, Denial
Can't believe what is
happening

Cataclysm of Emotion
Fear/Terror
Anger/Rage
Confusion/Frustration
Shame/Humiliation
Guilt/Self-Blame
Grief/Sorrow

Reconstruction
Time begins anew for
victims as they start life
after the trauma.

National Organization for Victim Assistance

As you can imagine, your body has been through a tremendous trauma.
The adrenaline pumping into your system alone can cause a great range
of emotional and physical responses. No doubt you are exhausted. It
is common to experience severe exhaustion after any trauma or crisis
event. What goes up must come down, and this is your body's natural
way of coming down from this heightened experience. In the upcoming
days, weeks, and even months, your body will be recuperating from this
experience. This is not something that happens overnight. Be mindful
that you may feel out of balance for a long time after this event. You will
experience a wide range of emotions, and it is important to identify them
and understand them. In Chapter Five you will focus on your feelings and
identify them one by one. But for now remember that feelings come and
go, and they will pass. Feelings cannot kill you, even though sometimes
they are so overwhelming that you may feel you cannot get through
them. Trust that you can, and know that this, too, shall pass.

AFFIRMATION

Right now I am experiencing a roller coaster of feelings, and I am overwhelmed. Today I know that feelings cannot hurt me, and I know that this, too, shall pass. Today I will be patient with myself and allow the feelings to come and go, trusting that they will pass soon.

When feelings rise in us and take over, there are many things we can do to tame them. First and foremost, remember to breathe. Take ten deep breaths in through your nose and out through your mouth. This will help to clear your mind, provide oxygen to your brain, and slow down your heart rate, while allowing you to feel whatever it is that is coming up for you. If the feelings are overwhelming, try writing about them in a notebook or journal. Call upon one of your support people at this time—maybe you need to talk to someone, or maybe you need to go out and do something physical to get the feelings out.

Common reactions to trauma

- Guilt and self-blame
- Mood swings and irritability
- Insomnia or bad dreams
- Loss of appetite
- Distressing memories about the event

- Anxiety and edginess
- Feeling disconnected or numb
- Withdrawing from others
- Difficulty concentrating
- Feeling sad or hopeless

EXERCISE

Complete the following statements. If you need more paper, use
your journal.

My physical reaction to this crime was
(Examples: My heart pounded, my muscles tensed up, I breathed faster
and harder, my hands or body trembled, I felt hot or cold, I froze, I ran,
I peed my pants.)

My emotional reaction to this crime was
(Examples: I was angry. I immediately began to cry. I became numb
or robotic. Shame, guilt. I am filled with rage. I am awakened
by nightmares.)

Today I feel my reaction was

No matter how you responded, no matter what you did or said, your
reaction was okay and normal for you. Everyone responds differently to
a trauma, but one thing you must continuously remind yourself is: *my
reaction to this abnormal event in my life was/is normal.*

Just as there is no "one size fits all" approach in recovery, there is no "one size fits all" approach to healing from trauma and victimization. Your reaction is unique to you, and while many people share commonalities in their responses, each person will have varying perspectives on how he or she feels and responds.

Remembering recovery basics

The acronym HALT (Hungry, Angry, Lonely, Tired) is commonly used in recovery to help us remember to tune into our emotional state of being. Sometimes we act or feel a certain way that is out of character for us, or that makes us feel out of touch with our normal responses. These are the times it is important to stop and try to figure out what is going on inside or around us. Sometimes it has nothing to do with anything other than that we might be hungry, angry, lonely, or tired. Once we can determine which one of these things we are feeling and address it, usually the feelings or actions we were engaging in subside. Self-awareness is key. It is vital to know and understand yourself in order to heal and stay in balance. So the next time you feel out of sorts, ask yourself these basic questions:

* What have I eaten today? Do I need to eat something?

* Am I feeling angry? Do I need to process something?

* Have I spent some quality time with people in the program lately?

* When was the last time I reached out to speak to someone in my support system?

* Am I getting enough sleep? Do I need to take a nap or change my bedtime to ensure I get enough sleep?

Nine times out of ten when you are not feeling like yourself, it is because of one of these culprits. These are areas in our lives where we can identify a need and fill it without too much effort. *Example: I am hungry; therefore, I will eat something so that need will be met, and I will immediately feel better in that sense.*

Trauma and the senses

In the moments and hours during a crime or trauma and after, many people experience heightened senses. We all have five primary sensory functions: sight, hearing, taste, touch, and smell. When a trauma occurs and we experience the rush of adrenaline pumping through our bodies, the five primary senses are usually heightened in some way. This means that one or more of our primary senses will seem very sharp, sometimes to the exclusion of all the other senses. A victim might say, "All of a sudden I smelled a strong odor," or "All I remember is seeing an explosion—the fire was so high and so bright," or "I just remember the cold feeling of the gun pressed against my back." It is common to focus on one sense or to remember only one key element of the crime in vivid detail.

It is critical for your emotional healing that you understand your response so that you can prepare yourself for how you will respond to certain triggers or reminders in the future. Just like we have triggers in our addiction—things that remind us vividly of how we used to feel when we used or wanted to use—you will now have triggers regarding this victimization.

Triggers are emotional reminders of an event or thing. They can creep up and send us into turmoil or right back into the feelings, thoughts, and reactions of a particular event. Think for a moment about what your triggers are when it comes to your addiction. What are the feelings, thoughts, events, people, and places that make you want to engage in addictive behavior?

Here are some examples of triggers, and then empty spaces for you to fill in your own. Examples of emotional (feelings) triggers include anger and hurt. Thought triggers may be reliving the event or thinking about going to court. Event triggers may be anniversary dates of the crime or court dates. People triggers may include anyone involved in the criminal case, such as the media or certain friends or family. Examples of place triggers are the scene of the crime, the courtroom, or the police department.

ADDICTION TRIGGERS

Feelings	
Thoughts	
Events	
People	
Places	

TRAUMA TRIGGERS

Feelings	
Thoughts	
Events	
People	
Places	

Triggers are like mini-storms in our path; they will pass, and the damage left depends upon our planning and response.

You cannot avoid triggers altogether, but the more prepared you are, the more easily you will be able to walk through them and make it to the other side with little to no additional emotional or physical harm to yourself.

Preparing for triggers

Revisiting and understanding your triggers will help you to prepare for when you encounter them. The best defense against something is a solid offense, and the best preparation is knowledge and understanding. The more we understand ourselves, our reactions, and our triggers, the better we can predict and prepare our defense against them. This process will help you have a better understanding of things, people, and places to avoid to safeguard your recovery and your emotional well-being as you heal from this crime. The more prepared you are, the easier tough emotional situations will be, since you cannot avoid life's twists and turns. You are striving to avoid getting spun out in the process of the twists and turns.

Now that you have identified your triggers, think about a scenario that you know will occur in the upcoming days, weeks, or months that could possibly be a trigger for you. Maybe it is attending a hearing for the offender in your case, or seeing an unexpected article in the media about the case. Maybe you know you have to go to a location that could be a potential trigger. Whatever the situation may be, I want you to think about how you will handle it, and what you can do today to put a plan in place that will allow you to avoid the revictimization or retraumatization that could occur. If you are alone, what can you do that will help you cope with the situation you've experienced? What things might you need in order to be okay in a moment when a trigger may affect you?

I know it is hard to plan for the unexpected, but the more you can think this through, the better position you will be in. Just as in recovery, we must know and understand how our addiction triggers could be engaged; we try to have a plan. Sometimes that plan is as simple as driving to a place ourselves so we can leave when we need to, or carrying a slogan, saying, prayer, or book with us that we can read to help calm us. Your plan may be to have the phone number of a support person and a cell phone on hand to make a call when you need to, or to carry an MP3 player with calming music or your favorite author reading positive words, a photo of someone you love to smile at, or a pack of tissues to blow your nose with after a crying jag. Maybe your plan includes not being alone, and ensuring you have a person with you in case you cannot drive or function well for a little bit. Whatever it is that you think will help in a moment of sudden crisis caused by an emotional trigger, now is the time to think it through.

EXERCISE

Take a moment now to write out the things you feel would be helpful to you and that would enable you to cope more easily with a triggering situation. Write down what you need to carry with you to help ease your trigger and allow you to be as emotionally safe as possible.

Let's end this chapter with a meditation.

I may not have control over my current situation or my feelings toward it, but for today I do have self-awareness. I can control my surroundings, and I can be aware of my triggers. I can prepare myself. I am taking healthy, productive steps toward my own healing.

Take a moment to write here or on a separate piece
of paper, or just process out loud or in your mind,
a gratitude list.

What are three things you are grateful for today?

_____

_____

_____

_____

_____

_____

_____

_____

_____

_____

_____

_____

_____

_____

_____

CHAPTER THREE

Not in My Family!

How could this happen?

No, it isn't possible.

I just saw my son; he cannot be dead.

I cannot believe this happened!

This cannot be true.

This isn't real.

I am going to open my eyes and surely this hasn't happened.

When I wake up in the morning this will all just be a bad dream.

How did this happen?

How could I let this happen?

I cannot believe I didn't . . .

I cannot believe I forgot to . . .

These questions and statements are normal reactions and thoughts to experiencing a very abnormal event in one's life. Denial and shock are common reactions to being a crime victim. But just as denial hurt us in our addiction, it can halt our healing process as well. It is important to acknowledge that denial is real, and that acceptance of the reality of the situation is the first step to healing. We cannot move forward until we accept that the circumstances of our situations are real.

First and foremost, you couldn't possibly have controlled this experience. You are not at fault in any way, shape, or form. You cannot always predict when something is going to happen, and no matter how much you safeguard yourself, you cannot control another person's actions. So right now, please stop beating yourself up for things you think you should have done or for things you didn't do.

AFFIRMATION

Today I accept the fact that this crime has happened. I am not at fault for the act of violence that was perpetrated against me. I couldn't have done anything to affect the actions of another person.

You are not alone; millions of Americans become victims of crime each year, and they have all been through a process similar to the one you are encountering now. Self-blame will do nothing but add to your pain and suffering, so right now give yourself a break. Let go of all the "should'ves" and "could'ves"; they will only make you crazy.

Acceptance of my addiction was the first step in my recovery from the disease. Here is a part of my story of acceptance of my victimization.

When I was raped I felt incredible guilt and shame. I thought I had brought the rape on or invited it because I was drunk at the time. I thought that because I went out and got loaded and blacked out, it took away from my being a victim—that I participated in the crime in some way. What I had to remember was that no one, no matter what I do or say, has the right to violate my body. Every person in this country has the right to consent to sexual activity. If you do not or cannot consent due to intoxication, a person should not—and cannot legally—attempt to engage in sexual intercourse with you. Did I make poor choices in my careless drinking? Absolutely, and in my recovery process I have dealt with those actions by working the steps of my personal recovery program and by forgiving myself. But I know today that it is not my fault that I was raped.

Acceptance is the key to unlock the door to healing

Control is an age-old friend to addiction. Addicts often use control as a method to avoid dealing with the actual problems at hand. *If I could just drink on the weekends, it would be okay. If I only drink after 5:00 p.m., then I don't really have a problem.* Attempting to bargain our way through dealing with a tough issue only prolongs our suffering and deters our ability to start healing. Dealing with life on life's terms is something we must do in recovery to maintain our healthy lifestyles.

"I kept thinking to myself that I should have been able to do something. I beat myself up over something that I had no control over."

"If I had arrived ten minutes earlier, maybe I wouldn't have been there when the guy held up the bank."

"God, if you just give me one more day I could . . . ."

"If I let myself cry about this, then that means I am weak."

Remember during this process, just as in early recovery, to "let go and let God." You are not in control; surrender yourself to the fact that this crime has occurred in your life, and you will begin to move through it more effectively. When we accept something in our lives, it becomes real and we can begin to deal with the reality. It's normal to want to change the course of unpleasant events that have unfolded in our lives, but living in a place where this event didn't happen will only serve to emotionally harm you and those around you.

"And acceptance is the answer to all my problems today.
When I am disturbed, it is because I find some person, place,
thing, or situation—some fact of my life—unacceptable to me,
and I can find no serenity until I accept that person,
place, thing, or situation as being exactly the way it
is supposed to be at this moment."

Page 417, Alcoholics Anonymous, Fourth Edition

In recovery we are taught how important acceptance is in our everyday lives. It enables us to let go and let our higher power take over so that we may return to a calmer, more serene place in our emotional growth. It is crucial that you accept that you have been harmed, that you have been violated in some way by the victimization you experienced. Once you accept what has happened in your life, you will be free to move forward into your new normal—because after such devastation your life will never be quite the same again.

"I knew that just as I had accepted that I was an addict, I had to also accept that I was a rape victim. It was a new identifier that I had to own."

In the beginning, it may feel like every second of every hour is a reminder of the crime. Living one day at a time can mean truly living one moment at a time, and that is okay.

Moving out of denial and into a place of acceptance

"I walked around for days in disbelief; I kept waiting for the phone to ring and the bank to say that it was a clerical error and that my money was returned to my account."

In order to accept this event in your life as fact and prepare for the future, you need to understand exactly what happened to you. The following exercise will serve as a helpful tool in organizing your thoughts. This exercise—while imperative to your healing—can itself be an emotional trigger. It may be very helpful for you to do this exercise in the presence of a trusted advisor, sponsor, friend, or counselor. Before engaging in this next step, please take a moment to assess your emotional status:

* Will thinking in vivid detail about the crime or event harm you emotionally right now?

* Will reliving this experience set you back?

* Are you alone?

* Is doing this alone a safe thing for you?

If you are uncertain, I ask that you consult with a friend, sponsor, or counselor, as this process will bring up emotions you may not be ready for. It is similar to a Fourth Step in recovery, but can be more intense depending upon what was in your Fourth Step. In my Fourth Step I recounted my rape, which was a pivotal point of my addiction that I needed to expose and discuss. I consulted my counselor at the time and made sure I had her emergency phone number handy in case I needed it, and I also made sure I had an appointment scheduled with her following my work. These are things you may want to consider doing before moving on with this exercise. It may be helpful to have someone you trust do this exercise with you so you are in a safe place.

The last thing I would want is to further your emotional harm, so please, if you have any hesitation, reach out to someone and talk it over with him or her first. You can always come back to this chapter and this exercise; as stated in the beginning of this book, it is simply a guide to be used in whatever way works for you.

EXERCISE

Try to remember the crime itself. Close your eyes and take several deep breaths, in through your nose and out through your mouth. Do this ten times—ten deep, cleansing breaths in and out. Take yourself back to the crime and slowly allow yourself to remember what happened—as much of it as you can. You may have very little memory of it, especially if you were intoxicated at the time. That is okay. Just try to remember as much as you can and then write down your answers to the following questions. You may not have answers to them all, but try to remember specifics such as colors, songs, thoughts, feelings, and scents. These will help you to identify your new emotional triggers.

What did you see?

What did you hear?

What did you feel?

What did you taste?

What did you smell?

Are there things you cannot remember?

Is there anything else worth noting?

I want you to stop here and acknowledge that what you just did was huge. You just took a big step out of denial and into your healing by accepting what has happened to you. By giving yourself the ability to go back and relive these events, you are giving yourself valuable tools for your recovery and your personal growth. Give yourself a big hug, a pat on the back, or whatever feels good to you. Sometimes I find it soothing to pull my knees up to my chest and wrap my arms around myself and just pull myself into a big hug.

What you just did is brave and may have brought up a lot of emotions for you. Let them out. Let yourself cry if you need to, or scream, or whatever else at this moment you need to do to take care of the emotions you're experiencing. This work is hard, as it is meant to be. You may find yourself exhausted from the emotions you are stirring up by doing this work. Be aware of that, and let yourself feel whatever is coming up for you. You may also feel energized as you feed off the emotional energy of bringing all of this back to the surface. Your adrenaline may be rushing again, as it did the day of the crime. That is okay, too. It will pass. Just know it is normal and it is part of this process. You may feel relieved, as though a weight has shifted inside you. You may feel nothing at all. Regardless of what you're feeling or aren't feeling, remember, this is your journey, and you dictate the course. No one person's experiences or feelings are going to be exactly the same as another's. Follow the lead of your emotions; let them guide you through this.

Now you have information about how to predict and prepare for what some of your new emotional triggers may be. This information will aid you in the future when you have emotional responses to things, similar to your addiction triggers. For me there are certain scents that remind me of smoking crack, and I never knew this until I was in a restaurant kitchen and my friend was cleaning the stove and all of a sudden the smell hit my nostrils. I froze, and my entire body remembered exactly what those smells meant. It smelled like when I used. My heart began to pound in my chest, and my pulse quickened a bit. Suddenly I felt a panic attack coming on, and I couldn't move. It took me a while to recover from it, and when I did I was baffled as to what had just happened. That is what our addiction triggers are—those things that remind us of our using past. Knowing them helps us to prepare for our reaction to them. By knowing our triggers we integrate this preparation into our new life.

Now I want you to go back and look at what you wrote in the previous exercise, and then add to your list of emotional triggers. In addition to my example, here are some others that may help you to break down your written thoughts into specific triggers.

"I remember vividly the song that was playing over the speakers when the bank was being robbed, and now when I hear that song I am immediately transported back to the crime."

"I was robbed at gunpoint from behind at an ATM. The man told me to count to one hundred before I could turn around and go anywhere. It never occurred to me months later that when my children were playing hide-and-seek, I would get upset when they started counting. It just so vividly reminded me of the crime."

"When I was beaten and raped by my boyfriend, there was a candle burning in the room. I always burned candles so the house would smell nice for him. It was a French vanilla scent, and to this day anytime I smell French vanilla, I get sick to my stomach."

EXERCISE

My emotional triggers are

What are three things you accept today as reality in relation to this victimization? What does it mean for you to fully accept this event in your life?

If you have completed this chapter, pat yourself on the back. It takes courage to move out of denial and into a place of acceptance. In the promises of the book *Alcoholics Anonymous*, we are told we will neither regret the past nor wish to shut the door on it. In this chapter, you opened the door to the reality of what happened to you, and now you are in a position to better prepare yourself for the events and emotions to come.

I want you to give yourself a lot of credit for doing this today. If you weren't able to identify all of your triggers, that is okay. This is a work in progress, and there is no real beginning or end point. Like recovery, your healing from this crime is a lifelong process. When you remember things, come back and fill in the areas you left blank. Strive daily for progress, not perfection.

By identifying your emotional triggers, you may have triggered aspects of your addiction. For many of us in recovery, emotions alone can be our biggest triggers. So now it is important to deploy some of your recovery tools. Go to a meeting, call your sponsor, call someone in your support network, write, run—do whatever it is you do to help your recovery. And best of all, know this: feelings are just feelings and they will pass just like the day.

Let's end this chapter with the following affirmation:

I am a strong person, and I have the ability to overcome anything in my life as long as I have the tools to understand myself.

Take a moment to write here or on a separate piece
of paper, or just process out loud or in your mind,
a gratitude list.

What are four things you are grateful for today?

_____

_____

_____

_____

_____

_____

_____

_____

_____

_____

_____

_____

_____

_____

_____

_____

_____

CHAPTER FOUR

If I Can Just Trust and Believe...

For many people, there is a huge loss of trust after victimization. Sometimes it can feel as though there isn't a person in the world you can trust anymore—including yourself. Learning to trust again is going to be a long process, but a necessary one if you are to fully recover and feel confident in yourself once again.

After my victimization it was hard for me to not feel as though I had been abandoned by my higher power. I had so much anger toward what I believed was an entity that should have protected me. Questions such as "Why me?" "Where were you when I needed you?" and "Why did you let this man hurt me in this way?" rose to my tongue with bitter resentment. Confused and needing something or someone to blame, I would lash out upward toward my higher power.

In the aftermath of trauma, many of us feel a crisis of faith and a great emptiness inside because what we once thought we knew of our faith has been challenged in ways we never imagined. Nothing makes sense, and instead of turning toward our higher power for solace, we may turn away, whether temporarily or for a long time. It's hard to trust and believe things will be okay after we've just experienced just how *not* okay things can be in our lives.

We know that in order to be successful in recovery, we must trust and believe in our higher power. The beauty of a recovery program is that we are able to define and shape our higher power to fit our own beliefs and ideals. After a traumatic experience it is easy to drift away from our higher power, and to not only question our beliefs but also lose our faith and trust in our higher power. The strong foundation you have built on your path of recovery may now be rocky at best, and reestablishing and identifying this connection with your higher power will help to smooth out that road once more, so you can walk with a steady step, and if you stumble and fall down, it will be there to pick you up and carry you.

AFFIRMATION

Today I will open my heart and mind to trusting myself once again. I will try to let go of blame, and trust in my higher power once again. If I do not have a higher power, I will attempt to discover a power greater than myself.

It may take a long time for you to feel like you can trust anyone again—yourself, others, or your higher power. This is normal after what you have been through. The following exercise is aimed at defining the concept of trust as it applies in your life today, and putting it into practice so you can begin to trust and believe again. Answer the following questions to get a better understanding of where your trust levels are today.

EXERCISE

What does trust mean to you?

☐ Yes ☐ No **I trust myself.**

> If you answer yes, explain what this trust in yourself means to you.

> If you answered no, what do you need in order to feel like you can trust again?

Things you can do to reconnect to your spiritual side

Meditation

Try to set aside at least five to ten minutes to be still and quiet. Relax your mind and body. Focus on your breathing; breathe deeply into your nose, allowing the air to flow into your stomach and fill it up like a balloon, then release through your mouth. Do this at least ten times in a row. Deep and cleansing breaths can allow you to let go of all the toxic energy you have stored in your body. The stale air you have been holding inside will be expelled back into the world. Clear your mind and try to be still for as long as you can.

Prayer

The value of positive thought has wonderful effects on emotional balance. If you have a religious background, find a particular prayer to start or end your day with. Many people find the Prayer of St. Francis to be beneficial, while others who are nondenominational turn to the Serenity Prayer or other prayers in twelve-step programs such as the Third- or Seventh-Step prayers. Sometimes the simple act of reciting something positive out loud or in your head a few times can completely change your frame of mind.

In recent years the power of positive thinking has gotten a lot of attention with books like *The Secret,* and there is true, meaningful power in positive thought. If you are struggling through the day, stop and drop to your knees and turn it over to your higher power, or pull out a poem or phrase that makes you smile and that allows you to refocus on positivity. Whatever you may be struggling with, get it out of your head. Try to verbalize it and give it up.

It is common to feel resentment and anger toward a higher power, whether or not you have a solid understanding of who or what your higher power is, and even if you do not believe in one. Victimization or trauma can bring about questions and thoughts like "How could God have allowed this?" "Why didn't God stop this?" "Where was my higher power when I needed him/her?" "My higher power abandoned me." It is normal to have your faith shaken after a traumatic event unfolds in your life. Be gentle with yourself and with your higher power. This is a process, and just like recovery it is all about progress, not perfection. Setbacks are just ways for us to grow into a better understanding of ourselves.

Developing connection with your higher power

In order to connect to a higher power we need to identify for ourselves what our higher power is and what it looks like. Your relationship with your higher power may be on solid ground, and if so, that is great. Remember, faith needs to be an action word in your life; it cannot be a static concept. Just like in our recovery program, we must do footwork in order to achieve the results and outcomes we desire. Faith, trust, and belief in ourselves are no different—we must do the footwork to obtain these.

The following exercises will help you to either shape your understanding of your higher power or remind you what you have and help you build upon it.

EXERCISE

In my life I trust (list people or things you have trust in)

I believe in

My understanding of a higher power is

In order to recover from anything, we must first believe we can. Believing that you can heal emotionally from this victimization is crucial. But that belief often comes from our faith in something greater than us. Now that you have defined what your understanding of your higher power is, let's go one step further and figure out how to access this source of strength and comfort. Sometimes when bad things happen it is easy to turn off our feelings, to turn away from that which will help us—in this case, our higher power and our spiritual base in our recovery. Understanding the importance of this belief will aid in an overall feeling of hope. Knowing there is a source of strength for you outside of yourself is a powerful tool. The following exercise will guide you through a better understanding of where you are with your higher power and level of belief.

EXERCISE

☐ Yes   ☐ No   **This crime has affected my relationship with my higher power.**

If you answered yes, explain how it has affected your relationship.

If you answered no, explain.

☐ Yes   ☐ No   **I have total faith in my higher power.**

If you answered yes, explain how you will put this faith into action.

If you answered no, explain what would help you to regain or gain this faith.

☐ Yes ☐ No **This crime has changed how I feel about my higher power.**

If you answered yes, explain these changes in detail.

☐ Yes ☐ No **I believe my higher power can heal my pain.**

If you answered yes, explain the steps you need to take in order to have this happen.

If you answered no, explain what you feel would work in the absence of your connection to a higher power.

Turning our will and self over to a power greater than ourselves is such an amazing and important part of surrender and healing. In order to accept your circumstances, which you have worked on in previous chapters, you must be able to trust and believe that you will be okay, that you will be provided for, and that you will get what you need in order to move forward. Rarely do we always get what we want in life, but if we trust and believe in something greater than ourselves and we act in accordance with this trust and belief, *we will always get what we need.*

AFFIRMATION

My higher power, I trust you wholly with my pain. I believe in you and your ability to remove my pain if I am able to trust in you enough to release it to you. Today I will turn my pain over to you and believe that you will give me what I need to get through today.

What does "turning your will over" look like for you? Is it prayer, meditation, writing, attending a meeting, a support group? One of the setbacks we often encounter in recovery is taking our own will back and trying to control everything around us. It is common to feel out of control after being a victim of a crime. Regaining that control is important for us to find a harmonious balance again, but we also know that seeking control in our addiction recovery can be a negative thing, as it can allow our self-will to run riot. Our challenge is to figure out a way to balance our need to be in control after the trauma with our understanding that it is imperative to our recovery to relinquish control to our higher power. We achieve this balance by seeking a deeper understanding of our actions and recognizing when we are in need of that balance.

EXERCISE

What does the phrase "self-will run riot" mean to you in your life today?

☐ Yes ☐ No   Are there aspects of your life right now that are out
of control? Explain.

What can you do right now to bring back some balance into your life?

Since the crime, are there ways that you have been able to relinquish
control and trust in your higher power? List them here.

If you haven't been able to do this, what do you feel would enable you
to do it?

What does trusting in your higher power mean to you?

Emotional connection through meetings and support groups

For many people, meetings and support groups are places where trust and belief are born. If you regularly attend a recovery meeting or a self-help group, then you understand the emotional connectedness you can find in a room full of people who all share a common bond. Most recovery programs are built upon the belief that we can do together what we cannot do alone. Such meetings allow us to be heard by others and to hear others' experiences. While no two stories are exactly the same in recovery, we all share a common bond. The same can be said for victimization and those who have experienced trauma; after all, isn't the pain and suffering we inflicted upon ourselves in our active addiction trauma in and of itself?

The power of two or more people gathered in any location for the purpose of sharing experience, strength, pain, and hope can be where the first seeds of trust and belief are planted.

EXERCISE

What is your current pattern of attending meetings or support groups?

How do you see meetings or support groups helping you to trust and believe again?

In what ways do you trust and believe in your program of recovery?

How can you apply these same program principles toward your emotional healing from this trauma?

Do you have any resistance to or fear of trusting and believing you can heal from this trauma?

It is okay to feel like you cannot turn this event over to your higher power, or to feel like you cannot trust and believe in anything right now. This chapter is but a guide in your process of trying to slowly let go and let your higher power back into your life. However, this is a long and painful process that you may not be ready for yet. If you had a hard time completing the exercises in this chapter, come back to it again and again until you are able to write something under each question. This is a lifelong journey, and you are not expected to simply pick up this book and move through these exercises with ease. It is only with time, and eventually trust and belief in yourself and something greater than yourself, that you will be able to regain the balance that was taken from you.

AFFIRMATION

Just for today, I will try to trust myself enough to allow trust in a higher power. Just for today, I will believe in something.

Take a moment to write here or on a separate piece
of paper, or just process out loud or in your mind,
a gratitude list.

What are five things you are grateful for today?

_____

_____

_____

_____

_____

_____

_____

_____

_____

_____

_____

_____

CHAPTER FIVE

Feelings Aren't Facts

Do you remember those feelings charts that were usually placed in day care and counseling centers? They displayed illustrations of faces, with the name of the feeling that corresponded to each facial expression listed underneath the faces, to help people identify their feelings. I am pretty sure that if someone placed one of those feelings charts in front of you right now and told you to circle what you are feeling, you would put one large circle around the entire chart. Or you would circle nothing because you are numb or simply unsure of what you're feeling.

It is normal to have your feelings all over the map after a victimization or traumatic event. Mood swings are common and can be hard to adjust to. But feelings aren't facts, and they will not kill you. As soon as you ride one out, another one will come in its place; sometimes it will be anger, rage, frustration, intolerance, and disdain, and then it may be restlessness, confidence, or another feeling. When you are experiencing intense negative feelings, it may be helpful to remind yourself of a saying common in recovery: *this too shall pass.*

AFFIRMATION

The feelings I am experiencing are normal, and they aren't facts.
They will come and go. This too shall pass.

And I promise you it will. No feeling will stay with you forever. You will most likely experience every emotion there is in the upcoming weeks, months, and years. The best defense against these emotional roller coaster rides, which are sure to come, is to have a solid offense. That means to learn and practice strategies to identify the feelings, to understand them, to process them to the best of your ability, to accept them without judging them, and to know that they will not last. This way, when a feeling comes smacking into your day and throws you off, you will at least be semiprepared for it and have a solid understanding of why it is happening and how you can manage it.

Feelings can be relapse triggers for people with addiction

In order to remain vigilant about your recovery but also give yourself the ability to feel what you need to feel, it is important that you truly understand why you're feeling a certain way and find ways to process the feelings appropriately. The only things a relapse into your addictive behavior of choice would offer you at this point are more pain, more suffering, and more emotional discontent.

There is no feeling that we can ever experience in recovery that our addictive behavior of choice won't make worse.

One of the most important things I want you to know is that no matter how you feel, it is okay. There is no rule book on how to feel about being victimized, and no one person will behave, respond, or feel the same way as another. Just as the feelings you had that were associated with the various stages of recovery are unique to you, so is this process. Do not let anyone tell you how you are supposed to be feeling. No one else can understand exactly what you are feeling right now. While people with shared experiences can certainly relate and understand the universal impact of trauma, no one knows what it is like to be you right now and to feel exactly how you feel. Again, be gentle with yourself. While it may feel like your feelings and emotions are out of control, you do have control over how you react to them. Knowledge is the ultimate power. This chapter is going to help you understand the various stages you may go through, the feelings you may experience, and ways to process those feelings in a healthy manner.

Grief and loss

By now you have probably heard of the five stages of grief and loss. In Elizabeth Kübler-Ross's book *On Death and Dying,* she first identified the five stages of the grief cycle. A person doesn't have to experience the stages in a particular order; however, the final stage is always acceptance. A person can reexperience any of the stages, and may shift back and forth among the various stages, experience a combination of them all at once, or experience them in a quick succession that comes and goes.

Kübler-Ross developed these stages by observing people who were dying, typically from an illness. While understanding the five stages of grief is a good and valid tool, in my opinion the process is a bit different for crime victims. Because Kübler-Ross's theory is based upon those dying from a disease, her stages are shaped more around grief and loss that aren't caused by another human being. Crime victimization and the grief that follows are always directly related to another person's actions, and this brings more questions, more anger, and possibly a longer period of grief. Without the horrific, careless, or intentional act of another person or persons, an individual wouldn't be a crime victim. Additionally, crime victims aren't prepared in any way for the trauma they endure. Crime victimization is a sudden, blunt force–type trauma that occurs without warning. Additionally, crime victims often endure media speculation, court proceedings where they must face the offender, and other events surrounding the crime for weeks, months, and sometimes years after the initial victimization. I believe this set of circumstances alters the stages for people, and I have taken the liberty of creating my own definitions that are more closely related to the reactions of crime victims who are grieving.

The first stage of grief is shock and denial. Shock and disbelief are the most likely the first feelings you will face because this is almost always the first way we deal with trauma, and any type of victimization can be classified as a significant trauma. It's kind of like the mind saying to itself, "If I don't believe it happened, then it really didn't." In extreme cases the mind will actually block out the memory of the event, which serves as a method of self-protection. Sometimes memories can stay dormant, buried in the mind for weeks, months, or years. This is why you hear of stories where people do not remember traumatic events until years later. For me, this happened with many of the details of the night I was raped. I knew it had happened, but I could not retrieve the details from my mind until I was in my twenties and I began having nightmares. The nightmares brought the details back into my consciousness.

The suppression of feelings is always associated with this stage, and there may be a sense of being numb or somewhat separated from the body. The shock/denial stage can last a long time for some crime victims; however, when an offender is apprehended and thrown into the criminal justice system, the reality of the event can sink in on you, the victim, more quickly as you are forced to deal with prosecutors, media, advocates, and so on, all of whom are solidifying the details of the crime for you. While the shock of the event can remain, it's harder to remain in denial when you are forced to begin dealing with the aftermath of the crime in intricate detail so soon via interviews and court proceedings.

As the shock begins to fade, you may experience a variety of strong, confusing feelings. They may include the following:

FEAR OR TERROR: This is to be expected after having your life and safety, and possibly your loved ones' lives and safety, threatened. You may begin to experience panic attacks, rapid breathing or shortness of breath, nightmares, night sweats, intrusive thoughts, and fears of being harmed again or of harm coming to your family or loved ones. These are all common emotional responses to trauma. While they may feel irrational at times, and you may even feel like you are going crazy, remember, you have been through a life-altering traumatic event. The fear will pass. Be gentle with yourself.

CONFUSION: *Why me? Why did this happen to my family? What did I do? What could I have done?* You will probably ask yourself these questions often, and unfortunately these are questions that rarely get answered for crime victims. It is sometimes impossible to understand the motivation for another's irresponsible and harmful act. You will begin to put back in place the pieces of the events that occurred, and you may be able to fully explain what happened—but you may never understand why. Additionally, you may have no memory of the event due to blackout or memory loss. For those who cannot remember, confusion can be extremely upsetting and frustrating.

FRUSTRATION: Frustration often results from feelings of helplessness and powerlessness during the crime. This is especially true if you were not able to fight off the offender or run away or call out for help. This frustration may continue during your journey into the criminal justice system, since that can be a very confusing and frustrating process.

Please utilize this book as a tool to take your first steps away from this frustration. In the following chapters you will learn all about your rights as a crime victim and how to navigate the criminal justice system so you aren't feeling so lost.

GUILT OR SELF-BLAME: It is common for victims to be consumed with guilt and to blame themselves for somehow playing a role in the crime, especially for those who were engaging in addictive behaviors at the time of their victimization. For example, you may think, "I was in the wrong place at the wrong time, so it was my fault," or "If only I hadn't been drinking or using, this would not have happened to me." The most important thing to remember is that you cannot control or predict the actions of another person. Yes, there are lots of safety tips and planning tools you can use to try to prevent crime. When we are actively engaged in our addiction, we aren't thinking properly; we aren't making solid decisions on our own behalf, and sometimes as a result of those poor decisions we end up in situations that we wouldn't otherwise be in.

Please remember that no matter what you were doing, what you wore, how you behaved, what you said or didn't say, whether you were blacked out, or whatever it may have been—**no one has the right to violate you. No one has the right to do you harm.**

AFFIRMATION

I did not bring this crime on myself, no matter what I was doing or not doing at the time the crime was committed. I cannot control the actions of another. I am not to blame for someone else's violent behavior. I have the right to live with the freedom from harm. Nothing I do or say gives another person the right to hurt me.

Self-blame is especially common when no offender is found. We may need someone to blame, so when no offender exists we turn that inward on ourselves. Some victims feel guilty if they think they should have done something differently while the crime was happening, such as yelling for help or running away. But remember what we learned in the beginning of this book: we have no control over what our bodies do when a crime is happening. Some people experience "survivor guilt," which is a feeling of guilt that they survived while someone else was injured or died.

SHAME AND HUMILIATION: Some victims may think that they "deserved" to be hurt. Some offenders try to degrade the victim on purpose by making them do things that are embarrassing, especially if the crime involves sexual acts. These types of offenders are more into power and control; they get off on the fact that they can make a person do things they know that they would never otherwise engage in. Rape, for example, can leave long-lasting feelings of being "dirty," and those feelings won't simply wash away. In a rape where the offender is known to the victim and may be a trusted friend or family member, this only compounds the feeling of being betrayed by those we cared for or trusted. It can also add to feelings of shame, because it is so easy to beat yourself up by questioning everything when you know the offender. Thoughts or questions like "I should have known," "I thought I knew him better than that," and "How could I not have known he would hurt me?" will only cause you more emotional pain, as you cannot answer them. There are no answers to these questions because the reality is that you could never have predicted this would happen. Repeat the previous affirmation.

SADNESS AND SORROW: Intense sadness is often the most powerful long-term reaction to a crime. The immediate feelings of grief and sorrow can stay with you for a long time after a crime occurs, and for many can lead to depression. It is important to monitor these feelings closely, as depression can be an especially dangerous place for an addict. If you already suffer from depression, as many addicts do, please consult your primary care physician or counselor so that together you can formulate an action plan to ensure your depression doesn't worsen.

No matter what trauma you have suffered through, there is likely to be a period of grieving. If you've lost a loved one, this period may be the longest for you, and the hardest. The sudden and traumatic death of a loved one baffles the mind; it is something that is never supposed to happen, yet it does. Coping and dealing with this excruciating loss is too difficult to try to put into words. The loss is so hard to define and explain. When someone dies from cancer, there is a process, there is usually some time to understand, and, while it is horrifically painful, it is expected. When you are smiling next to your loved one in a car and the next moment a drunken driver hits you and kills that person, there is no time for understanding or preparation. The emotional blunt-force trauma one experiences when a life is taken as a result of a chargeable criminal offense is beyond comprehension, and, in my opinion, this is the worst form of loss there is.

Depending upon your circumstances, a grieving period can last a few days, weeks, months, or even years. When grief rushes in, it challenges every aspect of our normal emotional state of being. It throws us completely off balance. It is important that you understand the feelings you are going to experience to the best of your ability so that you can learn to manage them. The only way to understand them is to feel them. You must feel your feelings. You also have to let them out. They can be like caged animals living inside you, and they can come out in dangerous ways if you do not process them and let them out.

In the next chapter we will go into more depth about shame, anger, and depression—the greatest enemies of recovery. Relapse often results from untreated depression and/or unresolved anger. It is critical to stay on top of your emotional state at all times. It may be helpful to keep a feelings journal. Each day try to acknowledge where you are emotionally. You can also use a calendar, or whatever method helps you to chart your emotions and keep yourself in check.

It can be as simple as this:

> Today I feel _____ (mad, happy, numb, tired, frustrated, confused, and so on).

I believe emotional awareness is the greatest tool in recovery. When you are checking in with yourself emotionally on a daily basis, it enables you to be one step ahead of your addiction, it enables to you to better predict and prepare for what you need to do for yourself to ensure you are okay on any given day.

Acceptance is the final stage of grief, although a person can go back to any of the other stages. This is when the person is able to acknowledge that the event will happen or did happen, that it isn't a good or bad thing, and that the person isn't a good or bad person for experiencing it. It can be a painful and difficult place to get to, but it is always an acknowledgment of great personal growth once achieved. It's easy to know when you are there because there is a sense of calm and peace that you begin to feel.

Take a moment to write here or on a separate piece
of paper, or just process out loud or in your mind,
a gratitude list.

What are six things you are grateful for today?

_____

_____

_____

_____

_____

_____

_____

_____

_____

_____

_____

_____

CHAPTER SIX

Shame, Anger, and Depression—Recovery's Greatest Obstacles

Shame and anger can be the two biggest barriers to recovery and to an effective healing process, and you are likely to be experiencing these two emotions on some level as a result of a victimization you have experienced. According to Brené Brown, PhD, LMSW, author of many books on shame and a research professor at the University of Houston Graduate College of Social Work, shame is experienced in the exact same manner as trauma. Shame is defined as the intensely painful feeling or experience of believing we are flawed and therefore unworthy of love and belonging. Shame often accompanies victimization; it is a way in which we make the crime more personal and define ourselves by it. This is particularly true of crimes that are sexual in nature.

Shame tells us that we are bad, when in reality something bad happened to us. Shame tells us we are flawed, when in reality it was the crime itself that was flawed. Shame tells us that as a result of the crime we are bad people, when in reality the person who committed the crime is the bad person—not us. Shame is a trap. It is a steel barrier that can prevent us from moving forward, from forgiving ourselves, and from understanding that we are not the crime that happened to us. Shame makes us feel like we are the crime.

AFFIRMATION

This crime does not define me. This crime is something external that happened to me; it does not own me. I am not a bad person. Something bad happened to me that was beyond my control.

Shame lives in the same manner as our addiction; it breeds on secrecy, silence, and judgment. Just as we have done in our recovery from addiction, we must shatter the silence, eliminate the secrets in our lives, and release ourselves from internalized judgment. The most important thing I learned in my early recovery was that my secrets would keep me sick. I knew that if I continued to hold on to the feelings of shame I had surrounding being raped, I would use again. Shame and addiction go hand in hand in this way, as they require you to keep those secrets in the darkest places of your spirit. It is only when you expose those secrets to the light of day that they dissipate. Light always drives out dark, and honesty and vulnerability are the cornerstones to healing. Remember, no one ever died from telling a personal secret or exposing a weakness; in most cases people were made stronger by doing so.

I remember in early recovery I was so scared to share my darkness and expose my secrets because I didn't believe anyone could relate. I couldn't fathom that anyone had done what I had done. I was wrong every time. Every time I opened up to someone I trusted and shared of myself, I was amazed that they had either done something similar or had felt and thought the very same things I had. This helped me to understand that I was not alone.

It is hard to eliminate shame from our lives because in order to do so we must expose the darkness; we must walk through the crime and the trauma to reach the other side. I wish there were a magical map to healing, but there is not. When we revisit the crime itself, we are in essence retraumatizing ourselves. We must be engaged in this process of remembering and accepting so we do not relapse or enter into an emotional downward spiral, which can easily happen when we reexperience the trauma, the pain, and other emotions we felt during the crime. We must stay aware of our emotions at all times, knowing that it is normal that we are feeling everything again and that it will indeed pass. It is easy to avoid dealing with our shame and anger because it is painful to have to relive the trauma and feel the feelings associated with it; however, we must feel in order to heal. We must work through the shame to eliminate it in our lives.

I recently interviewed Debra Puglisi Sharp, a survivor who has lived through hell. She is the author of *Shattered: Reclaiming a Life Torn Apart by Violence.* Here is what she had to say about shame and the role it played in her life:

> When my husband was murdered, my first task in psychotherapy was to forgive myself, as I felt "survivor's guilt." I was the intended victim. My husband's murderer confessed that he had been looking for a woman to kidnap and rape. As I worked in the garden on that spring day in April of 1998, a crack cocaine addict slipped into an open door in the back of my home. He waited for me, watching me from a window in my kitchen. My husband of twenty-five years, Nino, returned home from work. After he and I had a brief conversation, he entered our home and was fatally shot. For many months I blamed myself for Nino's death. It was not supposed to happen that way! My psychologist specialized in post-traumatic stress disorder. She desperately tried to explain that I was not

responsible for my husband's death. How was I to know that this man was in our home? Then I blamed myself for not locking the sliding door where our offender had entered. Again, I had to forgive myself for forgetting to lock one door . . . in the middle of the day. I thought it was locked, but when you have two cats that go in and out, it is easy to not check your door every time.

My second task was to rid myself of the shame of being repeatedly raped by my husband's murderer. I remember saying to my psychologist, "How can any man ever want me?" I felt dirty and unworthy of being with another man. My husband's body was still warm, and I am having intercourse with the man who murdered him. Of course, my thinking was not rational. It was rape. Again, it was NOT my fault. I needed to stop blaming myself. I learned that there are millions of women who are raped and unable to move on with intimate relationships. Fortunately, with excellent counseling and the support of a good man, I learned that rape is about power and control. I did not ask for this to happen. Once I was able to gain control of my life, I realized that if a man did not want me because of my victimization, he certainly was not worthy of me. The man who supported me then became my second husband. Not once has he ever treated me like a tainted woman. In fact, he joined me in several counseling sessions because he cared enough about our relationship to learn how a woman who has been raped feels. We celebrated our ten-year anniversary in July of 2010. The shame is history.

Debra's ability to identify her shame and work through it to regain control of her life is both inspirational and amazing. She rightfully had a ton of shame and anger.

Now let's take a look at any shame you may be dealing with. Shame likes to hide behind the shadows; it can act as a deception just like our disease, and its only way to stay alive within you is for you to keep it inside. As I said before, our secrets will keep us sick. Shame often masks itself as a secret inside of us, and if not addressed this can lead to self-destruction and possibly relapse. Shame and guilt can feel interchangeable. You may feel guilty about certain things and not realize that the guilt is what is causing the shame, or vice versa. In recovery it is vital to tell our secrets, and this holds true for the shame you are feeling. Name the shame. Get it out of your mind, body, and soul so it no longer holds any emotional power over you.

EXERCISE

Try to articulate what you are feeling ashamed about.

Do you feel any guilt?
What are you feeling guilty for?

Is there something specific you feel utterly ashamed about, and if so, what is it and why do think you feel this way?

Expressing anger

"I couldn't let go of my desire to hurt the man who harmed my child. I felt that if I let go of my anger, then I wouldn't have anything left to validate what had happened."

"I kept lashing out at my husband after the rape. It was like no matter what he did, it wasn't right, and I would get angry and yell at him. I didn't even realize I was displacing my anger at my offender onto him."

While anger is a valid and important part of our grief process after victimization, it can be a strong trigger for those in recovery, so you must deal with it carefully in order to prevent old patterns from emerging. Wanting to lash out at the person(s) who harmed you or your loved one is a common and understandable feeling. Learning how to process anger in a healthy, nondestructive way is the key to sorting out our feelings without reverting to addictive behaviors.

It is easy to give in to anger and allow it to overtake our emotional well-being. I assure you that at some point anger will come up, regardless of whether there is someone to blame or not (for instance, if an offender hasn't been apprehended yet or is still unknown, you may seek someone to blame for your angry feelings). This anger may be directed at someone not even be associated with the crime. You might blow issues out of proportion or even unintentionally fabricate them in order to vent feelings that you are experiencing but that otherwise have no justification for coming out. This most often happens with those we are closest to or feel safe with. While it sounds counterintuitive, the age-old saying "We always hurt the ones we love" rings true, especially when we are dealing with anger, since it is so consuming at times. It's easier to lash out at those we feel will forgive us or will understand, or those who are simply the ones who are always there.

We need to be able to identify how we behave or react when we are angry if we are to understand our anger, and help those around us to understand it as well. When you are angry, do you yell, scream, and cry, or get quiet and isolate? Do you feel the urge to hit something? If we know how we behave when angry, then we can inform those around us and find ways to deal with our anger in a healthy way.

EXERCISE

I know I am angry when

While anger is a healthy response to trauma, it is important to handle it properly because, left unchecked, anger ends up being the single most common thing that takes people right back to their addiction. Everyone processes anger differently, and learning how you can express your anger in the most productive manner will remain a huge asset for you in your everyday life. The following are examples of methods that have been effective for many people to help in processing and expressing anger:

- Writing
- Running
- Lifting weights
- Counting to ten
- Screaming
- Crying
- Taking a brisk walk
- Taking deep breaths
- Hitting something, like a punching bag or pillow

Don't be afraid of anger, especially at this time in your life. Do whatever it takes without victimizing another to get the pain out of your body and put it into the universe where it can begin to dissipate and leave you.

EXERCISE

The best way for me to deal with my anger is

Anger, left unchecked and unresolved, can often lead to depression. If you aren't releasing your anger in a productive, healthy manner, then it has nowhere to go but inward, and when it is turned inside into our body, mind, and spirit, it turns into depression.

Depression

Depression is a common side effect of what you are experiencing, and in many ways, if you didn't feel some level of depression, there would be reason to be concerned. However, during the process of grief, if the feelings are intense, depression can be dangerous since a depressed person may try to hurt him- or herself. A skilled therapist will help you to determine whether you are going through appropriate levels of depression or if you are venturing into a place where medical intervention may be appropriate. Only you and your doctor or therapist can make this determination.

If you are having thoughts of hurting yourself, be sure to let someone know, and get the appropriate care as soon as possible.

Depression, sadness, hopelessness, and feelings of despair often follow the acknowledgment of victimization. It is necessary for your recovery to embrace your feelings and validate them, but also important that you do not allow yourself to be consumed by them. There may be days when just getting out of bed will feel like the hardest thing you've ever had to do. There may be days when you will feel like the crying won't cease. Remembering to put one foot in front of the other and walk through your feelings is going to be extremely important during this stage of your process.

Getting help for depression

"I didn't feel like people in the rooms could really understand what I was going through after my daughter was killed. I had to seek other outlets in addition to my daily recovery meetings to manage my feelings."

The place of medication in recovery has been long debated, with many different opinions expressed. There are some who feel any medication that alters a person's mood in any way violates the principles of recovery. Recovery is a personal journey, and while there are many road maps and principles laid out for us to follow in various books and meetings, we must define them to fit our own needs in a healthy way. It is important to determine your level of depression and whether or not seeing a medical doctor in additional to your regular recovery routine is needed.

In the immediate aftermath of a crime, your medical practitioner may advise that you are in need of an antidepressant or antianxiety medication, perhaps on a short-term basis. Be sure your doctor understands addiction so that together you can make the best decisions for your recovery and for your healing. If you and your doctor determine that medication is a necessity, make sure you follow your doctor's instructions and inform those around you that you are taking this medication and explain why. In recovery, accountability and honesty are our strongest weapons against relapse. Addictive thinking cannot live long where honesty and accountability are consistently implemented in our lives. If we stay one step ahead of our addiction, then we can do the hard tasks that it takes to overcome our feelings.

The rooms of recovery are wonderful places for us to talk about our addiction and to release our emotions. But sometimes after a victimization or trauma, we need more. It may not be appropriate to discuss the victimization in the rooms of recovery, especially in the detail that you need to in order to heal. Finding a good therapist and support groups in your local area will help in this regard. Ask your victim advocate if he or she has any recommendations for therapists, counselors, and/or support groups specific to your needs. Look online for supportive environments, groups, or chat rooms where you feel safe and comfortable to talk about the victimization. The rooms of recovery are an amazing resource for finding other people who understand what you are going through and can relate. Finding a group or a therapist who fully understands victimization and the specific trauma you experienced will offer you a supportive and healing environment.

Take a moment to write here or on a separate piece
of paper, or just process out loud or in your mind,
a gratitude list.

What are seven things you are grateful for today?

_____

_____

_____

_____

_____

_____

_____

_____

_____

_____

_____

_____

_____

_____

_____

CHAPTER SEVEN

Substance Abuse and Victimization

In recovery we know that there are certain factors that may lead
to a relapse. People, places, and things are the top three things
that need to be changed and/or avoided to prevent a relapse back
into active addiction. As I stated previously, understanding emotional
triggers and being in touch with feelings are invaluable in recovery—
emotional awareness is the most effective tool in preventing relapse.
Trauma, grief, and victimization are all significant triggers that may lead
one to engage in his or her active addiction. After all, for most addicts
picking up is a knee-jerk reaction. It is a common response to dealing
with stressors in our lives. We lost a job, we go get hammered. Someone
made us feel bad about ourselves today, so we go eat a bag of chips and
a pint of ice cream. It is a self-defeating cycle that is extremely hard
to break, mainly because it is so ingrained in our coping mechanisms.
Recovery is behavioral modification in its truest sense.

Learning to not pick up a substance or use a behavior to deal with life is
something that is a daily and sometimes hourly exercise in recovery.

Right now you may be facing some of the most horrific emotions you have ever had to experience. Victimization and trauma can be the worst stressors you will ever face in your life, and your recovery may hang in the balance. The choices you make can either help you heal and maintain a path of recovery or lead you right back down the path of darkness. The fact that you are reading this book is an amazing step in the right direction—the direction of healing. You can do this. You can face these feelings, engage whatever is ahead of you in this process, and continue to maintain your recovery. You have already taken some significant steps toward ensuring your recovery remains intact: you have identified supportive people and services in your area, and you have identified your new emotional triggers. These are two steps in protecting yourself and your recovery. Remember, you are no good to anyone else unless you are taking care of yourself.

A slip in recovery is avoidable, and relapse is part of active addiction, not a part of the recovery process. If you have relapsed already as a result of dealing with this tragedy in your life, you can forgive yourself now, and give yourself permission to be human. Wake up today and make the decision not to engage in negative coping mechanisms. It is that simple; the choice is in your hands.

Engage in activities that you know will protect your recovery today. Call your sponsor or the support person you identified previously. Even if you have nothing to say, make the call, just to be accountable each day to someone other than yourself. Maybe you're familiar with the feeling, from early recovery, that the phone can feel like it weighs one hundred pounds. With what you are going through, you may experience that again. In many ways you are back in early recovery, but now you are recovering from something different. Many people who have long-term recovery, which may include you, feel that they should be able to handle anything. You may feel that you have overcome so much in the process of recovery that you shouldn't be having such negative thoughts about reengaging in active addiction. This is a trap! Do not fall into it. You are not God, you are not perfect, and you are at times vulnerable to relapse just like any other person. I have seen people with twenty or more years of recovery relapse. We have all heard the stories of those who thought they were shatterproof falling into a million pieces and relapsing. You are not a brick wall of indestructible strength. So give yourself permission to be human and know that it is okay.

Showing emotions and engaging a grief process openly and actively is not a weakness, it is strength and an asset to your recovery. Avoidance and denial may feel like a much better option or a comfort, but all they really do is prolong your pain. Avoiding your feelings, the events you have experienced, and the process of healing is in many ways like using a substance or behavior addictively. In order to fully recover from anything you must walk right through it—you cannot outrun it, go around it, or avoid it. At some point you will run smack into it, and the pain will be greater.

Many people have been victimized by an offender who was under the influence of alcohol and/or other drugs at the time of the crime. This can create a whole other host of issues for those in recovery. Because we understand addiction so intimately, and in many cases we engaged in criminal behavior ourselves while active in our addiction, it can create an odd sense of understanding or even sympathy for the offender. Again, whatever you feel is okay. You are entitled to all of your feelings, and they are all valid. But just because you understand a factor of the victimization that happened to you doesn't make it okay or right. Substance abuse is never an excuse for criminal activity.

Here are some statistics that illustrate just how frequently substance abuse and victimization are intertwined:

- In 2008, 125 people were murdered in brawls due to the influence of alcohol, and sixty-eight people were murdered in brawls due to the influence of narcotics.

- Seventy percent of intimate partner homicide and attempted-homicide offenders used alcohol and/or other drugs during the incident, compared with fewer than one-fourth of the homicide or attempted-homicide victims.

- Victims of rape are thirteen times more likely to develop two or more alcohol-related problems and twenty-six times more likely to have two or more serious drug abuse-related problems than those who are not crime victims.

- About one in five victims of violence who perceived the offender to have been using alcohol at the time of the offense (approximately 400,000 victims per year) suffered a financial loss attributable to medical expenses, broken or stolen property, or lost wages—totaling an annual loss of $400 million.

If your victimization happened while you were engaging in your active addiction, you are not alone. Just as crime and addiction go hand-in-hand for offenders, so it is often the same for victims of crime. Remember this basic fact: you are entitled to live a life free from the threat of violence. It doesn't matter what you did, what you said, what you wore, what you drank, or what you were using—no one has the right to violate you. No one has the right to harm you or your family members.

I have worked with many families whose loved ones were in the process of purchasing drugs when they were killed. The public scrutiny and guilt these families have faced is unacceptable. It is an added layer of pain, guilt, shame, remorse, and heartache that they shouldn't have to endure. While it is important for people to take responsibility for their actions, it is also important to truly understand that violence isn't an acceptable response to any behavior or action.

In our society, for some reason, we place victims in categories, such as "true" victims or victims of circumstance, and we treat them differently. I have heard people say, "Well, she was buying drugs when she was attacked, so she isn't a 'true' or 'real' victim." We need to shed this discriminatory lens through which we see victims of violent crime. A person who is engaging in a nonviolent act and then is violently attacked is a true and real victim. Sometimes our circumstances and our choices lead us to do things that we may not otherwise ever consider doing. When we are living in active addiction, we are most vulnerable to poor judgment, faulty thinking, and bad decision making. We aren't thinking clearly, and therefore end up in situations that enable our addiction. This does not mean in any way, shape, or form that any of the above makes us fair game for violent criminal attacks. Yes, we need to be held accountable for our actions and behaviors, and recovery teaches us how to do that; however, that doesn't mean we deserve to be held at gunpoint, violated, assaulted, raped, harmed, or murdered.

We have a horrible pattern in our society of blaming the victims and not holding the offenders accountable enough. An act of violence against one is an act of violence against society, and therefore we should all be enraged when someone we know is harmed. We need to stop saying things like "Why was she there at that hour?" "Why did she go to his house?" "Why did that mother not hold her child's hand the whole time?" "How could that man have left his front door unlocked?" We have this need to evaluate the victim's choices rather than to simply put the blame where it needs to be—on the person committing the crime. I think this stems from our constant need to prevent crime and learn from mistakes. We all make mistakes, but that doesn't mean anyone should have a crime perpetrated upon them in order to learn their lesson.

We live in a society where one of the promises of life is that we will have the freedom to live without the threat of harm. While prevention is vital and we must be vigilant, we cannot stray from this guiding principle, because if we do, then we are a guarded society constantly on the defensive, and that is simply no way to live, in my opinion. We need to find a productive balance between prevention and holding offenders accountable, preferably one that refrains from blaming those who are harmed.

For many victims of sexual assault, substance abuse is a core factor. According to the US Department of Justice, Bureau of Statistics, in one out of three sexual assaults the perpetrator was intoxicated.

According to the World Health Organization, victims of sexual assault are

three times more likely to suffer from depression.

six times more likely to suffer from post-traumatic stress disorder.

thirteen times more likely to abuse alcohol.

twenty-six times more likely to abuse drugs.

four times more likely to contemplate suicide.

Whether it was the offender or the victim who was using at the time, it doesn't lessen the crime. Intoxication is not an excuse for criminal behavior, and in most states it cannot be used in court as a viable defense. Juries are often instructed to ignore the intoxication levels of both the victims and the offenders when it is being used as a defense; however, this doesn't stop attorneys from trying to pull the focus off of the crime and put it on the use of substances. Blaming the victim is a huge problem, and when substance abuse is involved it tends to become a larger factor than it should be.

I was raped when I was twelve years old, and I was drunk at the time. My offender was twenty-eight years old, and he was drunk as well. I carried guilt and shame around with me for many years, thinking that somehow I was to blame for the assault. The truth is that no one has the right to violate my body whether I am sober or drunk. When I finally went into treatment for my addiction many years later and learned about my disease, it helped me heal from all that guilt and shame. It wasn't my fault. The man who raped me suffered from a different disease, pedophilia, and it made me grateful that I was dealing with a disease that was treatable. In a strange way, understanding my own disease helped me to forgive my offender for his disease. It helped me understand that certain people are much sicker than others, and that certain diseases have no cure.

EXERCISE

Take a moment to think about the circumstances surrounding your particular victimization and answer the following questions.

Was your offender using drugs or alcohol?

If so, what are your feelings about that? Does it affect the way you view the crime?

Where you engaged in active addiction when the crime was committed?

If so, are you carrying around unnecessary guilt, blame, and shame about this?

AFFIRMATION

It doesn't matter what I was doing, where I was, what I wore, or how I behaved. No one has the right to violate me or my family. Intoxication is not an excuse for bad behavior. Today I will forgive myself. I understand that I have a disease and that, if left untreated, it will continue to occur in my life. Today I am committed to my recovery.

Take a moment to write here or on a separate piece
of paper, or just process out loud or in your mind,
a gratitude list.

What are eight things you are grateful for today?

_____

_____

_____

_____

_____

_____

_____

_____

_____

_____

_____

_____

_____

_____

CHAPTER EIGHT

Victims Have Rights?

"I had no idea that I had certain rights. When I found out that I did and hadn't been informed, it felt like a different level of victimization all over again."

Most of us know that we have the right to remain silent, the right to an attorney, and all the other constitutional rights that are afforded to those who are charged with a crime in our country. Just as the accused has a set of rights, so does the victim. The best way to begin to understand the process that you are about to be thrust into is to understand how the legal system works and who has what rights.

When a crime occurs, a police report is immediately filed by the responding officer. The officer you met should have given you copies of your rights as a crime victim, but don't be alarmed if he or she didn't; many forget or just do not provide this information. However, you are legally entitled to it.

Unfortunately there is an imbalance in the legal system when it comes to victims' rights. The accused has rights under various amendments in the United States Constitution—the ultimate authoritative document in our nation that affords us rights such as freedom of the press, the right to vote, and the right to bear arms. Crime victims, however, do not have rights in the United States Constitution.

The following are some of the constitutional rights the defendant in your case will be afforded:

Fourth Amendment to the US Constitution

The right of the people to be secure in their persons, houses, papers, and effects, against unreasonable searches and seizures, shall not be violated, and no Warrants shall issue, but upon probable cause, supported by Oath or affirmation, and particularly describing the place to be searched, and the persons or things to be seized.

Fifth Amendment

No person shall be held to answer for a capital, or otherwise infamous crime, unless on a presentment or indictment of a Grand Jury . . . nor shall any person be subject for the same offense to be twice put in jeopardy of life or limb; nor shall he be compelled in any criminal case to be a witness against himself, nor deprived of life, liberty, or property, without due process of law. . .

Sixth Amendment

(The Sixth Amendment is by far the most applicable in your case.)

In all criminal prosecutions, the accused shall enjoy the right to a speedy and public trial by an impartial jury . . . and to be informed of the nature and cause of the accusation; to be confronted with the witnesses against him; to have compulsory process for obtaining witnesses in his favor, and to have the Assistance of Counsel for his defense.

Fourteenth Amendment

Nor shall any State deprive any person of life, liberty, or property, without due process of law.

Read more at http://www.america.gov/st/democracy-english/2008/June/20080630231256 eaifas0.3084683.html#ixzz0q4jO6JHw.

As a crime victim, you have a plethora of legal rights. Unfortunately, most people have no idea these rights exist. It is important for crime victims to be informed of their rights and to know what to do when they are violated, as they often are, within the system.

Today we still have a system that caters more to offenders and forgets about the victims. Even though rights have been enacted, they have been in place only since the 1980s, so advocates are still working hard to ensure that people understand these rights and enforce them. The criminal justice system through the years has recognized that we do not have an equal playing field for both the accused and the victim of a crime. Offenders have the Constitution on their side, which is the single most powerful document in our country. Anything that comes after the Constitution, such as laws or statutes, always falls a bit below the Constitution in terms of authority. Amendments to the Constitution are the only true way to achieve equality within any given right in our country. There has been much debate and effort put into proposing a constitutional amendment that would include victims' rights, but until that day comes we must work with what we have, and an unfortunate result is that far too often a victim's rights are violated—many times without the victim even knowing it has happened.

Understanding what your rights are and when they come into play throughout the various stages of the criminal or juvenile system will help ensure that they aren't violated. Just as you had to learn a new set of guidelines and principles to sustain and maintain your recovery, now you must do the same regarding your victimization. The more information you have, the better you will be able to understand what is going to happen, what you can do about it, and what the possible outcomes will be.

> Thirty-two states have amended their individual constitutions to include rights for crime victims. They are Alabama, Alaska, Arizona, California, Colorado, Connecticut, Florida, Idaho, Illinois, Indiana, Kansas, Louisiana, Maryland, Michigan, Mississippi, Missouri, Nebraska, Nevada, New Jersey, New Mexico, North Carolina, Ohio, Oklahoma, Oregon, Rhode Island, South Carolina, Tennessee, Texas, Utah, Virginia, Washington, and Wisconsin.

Since each state has its own set of laws regarding crime victims, here I use the Federal Victims' Rights Act to establish a basic understanding of the rights you should be afforded in your jurisdiction. The Federal Victims' Rights Act governs any and all crime that would go to federal court rather than county or state court. These acts are things such as crimes that cross state lines, multiple offenses in multiple areas, or any crime that occurs on federal property, such as a national park. Many states have adopted laws that are similar to the federal act, but they all vary in many ways, so please check in your local jurisdiction to find out what your specific rights are, as they may be different from what is listed here. To find information in your state or county, please refer to the Office for Victims of Crime (OVC) at www.ovc.gov. There you can find out where to reach local services. The OVC was established by the 1984 Victims of Crime Act (VOCA) to oversee diverse programs that benefit victims of crime.

The Crime Victims' Rights Act of 2004, 18 U.S.C. § 3771, provides that officers and employees of the Department of Justice shall make their best efforts to see that crime victims are notified of, and accorded, the following rights:

* The right to be reasonably protected from the accused.

* The right to reasonable, accurate, and timely notice of any public court proceeding, or any parole proceeding, involving the crime or of any release or escape of the accused.

* The right not to be excluded from any such public court proceeding, unless the court, after receiving clear and convincing evidence, determines that testimony by the victim would be materially altered if the victim heard other testimony at that proceeding.

* The right to be reasonably heard at any public proceeding in the district court involving release, plea, sentencing, or any parole proceeding.

* The reasonable right to confer with the attorney for the government in the case.

* The right to full and timely restitution as provided by law.

* The right to proceedings free from unreasonable delay.

* The right to be treated with fairness and with respect for the victim's dignity and privacy.

If you are living in another country or you were a victim of a crime while on a cruise ship or on vacation in another country, you are also afforded certain rights. The most universal right is the right to compensation for certain losses and expenses associated with the crime.

Visit the Office for Victims of Crime's webpage at http://ovc.ncjrs.gov/findvictimservices/search.asp to find out what rights or services you are legally entitled to.

EXERCISE

As I stated previously, each state has a different set of victims' rights, and while the majority of them mirror the Crime Victims' Rights Act, some go above and beyond that and provide more rights, while others fall slightly short. Look up your state's or territory's victims' rights laws so you know exactly what rights to expect in your area. Familiarize yourself with these rights and services so you know what to expect and when to advocate for yourself and when to get help.

Take the time to print out the rights in your state or note them in your journal so you are fully informed. You may even wish to go through this chapter and highlight the areas that are applicable in your state and also note the areas that aren't.

As you move forward through the system, understanding the "key players" in your case will become a vital resource for you in terms of getting and receiving accurate and up-to-date facts about your case. Place the following information in your address book, cell phone, PDA, or whatever you carry with you on a daily basis so you have access to it at all times.

1. The arresting officer's name, phone number, and email, and the police report number.

2. The name, phone number, email, and address of employment of the victim advocate assigned to your case.

3. The prosecutor or attorney assigned to your case. (Sometimes this doesn't happen until a case is bound over for court, so you may not have this information right away, but find this person's contact information as soon as possible.)

4. Defendant or defendants in your case. If possible, find out their full name(s) (accurate spelling), date of birth, and any other identifiable characteristics you can. This will be helpful in referencing your case to various agencies or offices you may need to be in contact with, as often cases are listed by the defendant's name. (This is particularly important when wanting to receive notification of prison, jail, probation, or parole release.)

A victim advocate is someone who works either in the prosecutor's office or in an independent agency, such as a victim services organization, a domestic violence shelter, a rape crisis center, or a homicide survivor network. These are services that are funded by federal, state, county, and other public monies. Their services are free to you as a crime victim, and in most places they are confidential. Their sole purpose is to predict and prepare every step of the process for you. They are there to be a supportive ear and a helping hand to guide you through this process so you don't get lost along the way. Just as you turn to your sponsor in recovery on a consistent basis for support and guidance throughout your recovery, you can turn to your victim advocate in a similar manner. Utilize your advocate just as you would your sponsor; he or she is there to help. The more support you have around you and the more information that you are empowered with, the less likely you will be to fall back into old destructive patterns.

AFFIRMATION

I am not alone in this process. I have rights, and I am not completely powerless over the system I am about to engage in. I have people who will guide me. Just for today I will reach out my hand for help and accept the help that is offered to me.

Take a moment to write here or on a separate piece
of paper, or just process out loud or in your mind,
a gratitude list.

What are nine things you are grateful for today?

_____

_____

_____

_____

_____

_____

_____

_____

_____

_____

_____

_____

_____

_____

_____

_____

_____

_____

CHAPTER NINE

Where Do I Turn?
Navigating the Criminal
Justice System

When was the last time you went to your local courthouse? Do you know where it is located? Would you know where to go if you had to appear in court? The criminal justice process is arduous, and many people do not know how the system actually works. Now that you have been involuntarily thrust into this new process, it is important that you understand how it works and how to navigate it.

You may also feel that because of shows like *Law and Order* and *CSI*, you have a good working knowledge of the system. Please do yourself a huge favor right now and ignore everything you've seen on TV or in movies. The portrayal of the criminal justice system in TV shows and movies is grossly oversimplified and usually altogether inaccurate. While they are entertaining to watch, in the interest of time and drama these shows rarely depict what truly happens. Unless you spend countless hours watching truTV, you most likely have the wrong impression of the criminal justice system already.

The first thing you will notice is that there is a lot of "hurry up and wait." Some events in a criminal case have legal timelines and therefore will proceed in accordance with deadlines, but most of the time your case will be continued and held up in the court system for weeks or months, and in some cases even years. This is where a crime victim advocate comes into play and can be extremely helpful to you. Crime victim advocates help victims and their families by keeping them informed about the progress of an investigation, preparing them for trial, referring them to needed services, explaining court proceedings, and acting as a liaison with state and local agencies. By providing support to people who have been devastated by a crime, they free police officers and prosecutors from the task of dealing with distraught families and friends.

Crime victim advocates come from various parts of the system. Some victim advocates are based in the district attorney's office and work for the prosecutor's office, some work in police departments, some work for independent nonprofit victim service organizations such as the Victim/Witness Assistance Program or the YWCA, and some are attorneys or legal advocates.

The most important thing you can do is to educate yourself about how the system works so you are ready for each and every step. Below is the basic flow of a criminal investigation and prosecution provided by the National Crime Victim Law Institute.* I have included rights that you have at each step of the process, and an action plan for you to use to implement your rights. The steps involved in the investigation and

*This information is taken, in part, from the work of the National Crime Victim Law Institute (NCVLI), www. ncvli.org. NCVLI is a nonprofit organization committed to promoting balance and fairness in the justice system through crime victim-centered legal advocacy, education, and resource sharing. NCVLI is working to secure for every victim free or "low bono" legal services to protect their rights in criminal courts.

prosecution of a criminal case vary from jurisdiction to jurisdiction. Many of the stages identified here can recur throughout a criminal investigation and prosecution. For instance, in most jurisdictions a defendant may be released at any stage of the criminal prosecution.

I am not an attorney, so the following information should not be deemed as legal advice. Contact the National Crime Victim Law Institute at www.ncvli.org or 1-888-768-6556; they can offer legal assistance and referrals.

Common steps of a criminal investigation and prosecution
PREARREST INVESTIGATION

Prearrest investigation is the stage of a criminal procedure that takes place after a report of suspected criminal activity is made or law enforcement otherwise becomes aware of such activity, but before an arrest is made. The law enforcement agency investigates whether a crime has occurred and whether an arrest should be made. If the agency determines that the evidence uncovered during prearrest investigation reveals that a crime was committed and if a suspect is identified, it may arrest the suspect or, depending upon the jurisdiction, present the investigation results to the prosecuting attorney. If the jurisdiction is one in which the prosecuting attorney becomes involved before the arrest, the prosecuting attorney generally decides what, if any, charges to file; only after this determination does an arrest take place. Alternatively, after an investigation, law enforcement may determine that there is insufficient evidence to pursue the matter, and no arrest is made.

YOUR RIGHTS: *At this point you should have been made aware of your rights by the law enforcement agency; you should have been given a copy of your basic rights and information about victim compensation in your state. If you were not provided with this information, call the police department today and ask for it.*

ARREST

An arrest occurs when the individual accused of a crime is taken into custody by law enforcement. Generally, an arrest may be made in two ways: (1) If a law enforcement officer arrives at the scene of the crime and determines that there is probable cause for an arrest, the officer can take a person into custody immediately, or (2) The officer may make an arrest pursuant to an arrest warrant. The requirements for making a proper arrest and obtaining a warrant vary from jurisdiction to jurisdiction and often depend upon whether the crime is a felony or a misdemeanor.

YOUR RIGHTS: *You have the right to know when the accused is arrested, whether a bail hearing is scheduled, whether he or she was granted bail, whether he or she made bail, and his or her whereabouts. In some states you also may have a right to protection and the ability to talk about your protection needs at the bail hearing.*

A police officer, your victim advocate, or the prison should call you with this information immediately. Particularly if you are a victim of domestic violence or sexual assault, or if you are a witness to a violent crime and are concerned the offender may retaliate, you need to be made aware of the accused person's whereabouts so that you and your loved ones can create a safety plan that is appropriate for you.

A safety plan is something that you and your advocate can come up with together and may include the following steps to be prepared to get away:

1. *Keep with someone you trust a spare set of keys, a set of clothes, important papers, prescriptions, and some money.*

2. *Keep any evidence of physical abuse (ripped clothes, photos of bruises and injuries, and so forth).*

3. *Plan the safest time to get away.*

4. *Know where you can go for help; tell someone what is happening to you. Have the phone numbers of friends, relatives, and domestic violence programs with you.*

5. *Call the police if you are in danger and need help.*

6. *If you are injured, go to the hospital emergency room or a doctor and report what happened to you; ask that they document your visit.*

7. *Plan with your children and other family members, and identify a safe place for them—a room with a lock or a neighbor's house where they can go for help. Reassure them that their job is to stay safe, not to protect you.*

8. *Arrange a signal with a neighbor; for example, if the porch light is on, call the police.*

9. *Contact your local victim services program for more resources.*

Many states have a program called SAVIN, Statewide Automated Victim Information Notification, which is an automated system that you can access online to receive notifications regarding the custody status of your offender. You can be notified when he or she is transferred from one prison to another, when he or she is coming up for parole, and when he or she is coming up for release. To see if this service is available in your area, visit www.vinelink.com and click on your state.

INITIAL APPEARANCE

Generally, as soon as practicable following arrest, the accused must be brought before a court. At the initial appearance, the court informs the accused of the charges and advises the accused of his or her rights to counsel and to remain silent. The defendant may be released at the initial appearance.

YOUR RIGHTS: *Again, your rights would be to know whether the defendant has been released and the possible right to protection.*

GRAND JURY (NOT ALL JURISDICTIONS HAVE GRAND JURIES)

A felony case is usually commenced by grand jury indictment or a preliminary hearing, which is discussed below. If the case is instituted by a grand jury, the prosecutor goes before the jury to ask them to indict the accused. A grand jury is a group of private citizens who conduct proceedings, generally with jury members sworn to secrecy. The proceedings consist of the prosecutor presenting evidence and providing legal advice to the grand jury. As part of its investigation, the grand jury has the power to compel testimony, including the testimony of a crime victim. After hearing the evidence presented by the prosecution, and through its own investigation, the grand jury votes on whether the accused should be indicted or the case dismissed.

You have limited rights at this stage; grand jury testimony is always done in seclusion and is not open to the public, so you cannot sit and hear testimony as you normally would in open court. However, privacy, protection, and other rights still attach, and if you are required to testify you are entitled to some accommodations.

PRELIMINARY HEARING

A felony case may also be commenced by a preliminary hearing held within a reasonable time after the filing of the crime information. If the case is commenced by a preliminary hearing, the defendant has the right to be present and to be represented by counsel at the hearing. The prosecutor and the defense attorney can each present evidence at the hearing to establish or challenge whether probable cause exists to believe that a felony was committed, and whether it was committed by the defendant. This evidence can include testimony, including that of the victim. Generally, limited discovery is available to the defendant at this stage, and during the presentation of evidence the defense is generally allowed to cross-examine any of the state's witnesses, including the victim. If the court finds there is probable cause to believe a felony was committed by the defendant, the defendant is "bound over" for trial. A defendant may be released at this stage. If the court finds there is no probable cause to believe a felony was committed by the defendant, the court must dismiss the case and release the accused.

YOUR RIGHTS: *You have the right to be informed of the date, time, and location of the hearing and to be present and possibly heard there. You may be needed for testimony at this stage as well. In most cases your victim advocate will accompany you to the hearing. You have the right to be present for all testimony as well, so if the defense attorney attempts to sequester (meaning to keep you out of the courtroom until you testify), in almost all jurisdictions you can argue this with the judge.*

ARRAIGNMENT

After charges have been brought, whether by information provided to the courts via an arrest or hearing or grand jury indictment, the defendant is arraigned. At the arraignment, the defendant is formally informed of the charges and given a copy of the indictment or information, and enters a plea responding to the charges. A defendant may enter into a plea bargain at the arraignment, as the defendant has the option at any point to admit guilt, which would then allow him or her to take a plea. Even if a defendant does not enter a plea, he or she might be released.

Bail is a tricky subject and is handled differently by every judge. Basically, all defendants have the right to bail unless they have committed a chargeable offense that doesn't offer bail; for example, first-degree murder in Pennsylvania doesn't allow for bail. This rule varies from state to state, so check the law in your state. However, if the offense allows for bail, it should be set based on varying factors such as the defendant's ties to the community, flight risk, the severity of the crime, and the public's safety.

YOUR RIGHTS: *You have the right to be informed of the date, time, and location of this event, and you have the right to be present and* to be heard. If the defendant does enter into a plea deal or agreement, in most jurisdictions you have the right to first confer with the prosecutor as to your wishes for the outcome of the case before the plea is offered or finalized. Ultimately it is the prosecutor's decision how to resolve the case, but you have a right to voice your opinion to the prosecutor, and then, if you still disagree, directly to the court before the plea is accepted. If a plea is entered and accepted at this stage, the defendant could be sentenced as well.

If this happens, you have the right be heard at sentencing, or to "allocate." This generally means providing a victim impact statement. A victim impact statement refers to written or oral information about the impact of the crime on you and your family. Victim impact statements are most commonly used at sentencing. Such statements provide a means for the court to refocus its attention, at least momentarily, on the human cost of the crime. They also provide a way for you to participate in the criminal justice process. The right to make an impact statement generally is extended beyond the direct victim to homicide survivors, the parent or guardian of a minor victim, and the guardian or representative of an incompetent or incapacitated victim. This is the one time in the criminal justice process where you have a clear and strong voice in the courtroom. Your victim advocate can assist you in the preparation of your victim impact statement. Your statement can be submitted in writing or given orally, or both, to the judge. It should focus on the impact of the crime physically, emotionally, and financially. Your statement should be directed toward the judge, but you can make statements directly to the defendant as well. This is an important right to engage in, as it may present a healing component for you that you may not otherwise have. You may also want to make note to the court at this time of any restitution you wish to seek.

DISCOVERY AND MOTION PRACTICE

Discovery is the pretrial process by which the prosecutor and the defense attorney exchange information and material about the case. Discovery is an intricate process governed by each jurisdiction's rules of criminal procedure. It is important to remember that the criminal defendant has no constitutional right to discover information from the victim.

In addition to discovery, and often stemming from discovery, there is usually considerable pretrial motion practice. A motion is a paper filed with the court asking it to do something in the case. Motions by the defense may include motions to dismiss the indictment, to suppress evidence, or to introduce specific evidence at trial. Motions by the state may include a request for reciprocal disclosure or a request for the defendant to disclose an alibi or psychiatric evidence. A crime victim's attorney may also bring motions asserting the victim's rights. These may include motions to quash a subpoena, to protect a victim's identifying information, or to exclude the press from certain hearings.

YOUR RIGHTS: *You have the right to be informed of the date, time, and location of this event, and you have the right to be present and to be heard if any of your rights are at issue. Additionally, if you are a minor victim or a rape victim, you are afforded the right to have your identifying information protected by the court.*

PLEA BARGAINING AND ENTRY OF PLEA

Instead of going to trial, a defendant may plead guilty pursuant to a plea agreement. A plea agreement is an agreement that the defendant will plead guilty to the original charge, or to another charge, in return for a concession from the prosecutor. Typical concessions include (1) dismissal of other charges; (2) recommendation of a particular sentence, or agreement not to oppose the defendant's request for a particular sentence; or (3) recommendation for, or agreement on, another appropriate disposition of the case. After a plea agreement has been reached, the plea is presented to the court, and the court may do one of three things: (1) reject the plea agreement; (2) discuss alternatives to the plea agreement that are acceptable to the court; or (3) accept the plea agreement. If the court rejects the plea agreement, the defendant may withdraw the guilty plea.

YOUR RIGHTS: *You have the right to be informed of the date, time, and location of this event, and you have the right to be present and to be heard regarding your opinion of the plea. If the plea is entered and accepted by the court and sentencing follows, you have the right to give your victim impact statement. (See Arraignment for more information on your victim impact statement.)*

TRIAL

A trial is the proceeding during which evidence is presented and guilt is determined. A trial is held before a jury or, if the defendant waives the right to trial by jury or for certain misdemeanors, before a judge. A trial before a judge is called a bench trial.

YOUR RIGHTS: *You have the right to be informed of the date, time, and location of this event, and you have the right to be present. Additionally, you have the right to be informed of all testimony that the prosecutor will be presenting, you have the right to know about any visual evidence that will be shown to the jury, and you can request to see that evidence prior to trial. Many times 9-1-1 calls are played, and these can provide key evidence but also may be painful reminders for victims. Additionally, crime scene photos may be shown, along with coroner's reports in cases where someone was murdered. All of this evidence can be emotionally traumatizing for you and your loved ones. You have the right to ask the prosecutor to see and hear these pieces of evidence in advance so that you are not shocked or retraumatized in open court. If you do not wish to see or hear these pieces of evidence, you can request that the victim advocate or prosecutor inform you when they plan to present them so you can leave the courtroom. In most cases, you are free to get up and leave the trial at any point; the* *only time the court will close a courtroom, meaning you would not be able to physically leave the courtroom, is during opening remarks and closing remarks. Be sure to ask the prosecutor when he or she plans to display certain pieces of evidence, as sometimes they are used during opening and closing remarks.*

In terms of what the defense will present, you have limited rights. If they choose to use photos, phone calls, or similar evidence, you may not know about it in advance; however, in most cases the attorneys have conferred and the prosecutor knows what the defense plans to submit as evidence. There shouldn't be many surprises for you during trial if you are prepared properly by your victim advocate and the prosecutor.

VOIR DIRE

Voir dire is the process by which a jury is questioned and selected. In a capital case, voir dire is split into two phases: the death qualification phase and the general voir dire phase. General voir dire means all the potential jurors are brought into the courtroom at once and are questioned as a group by the prosecuting attorney and defense attorney. In the event of a capital case or death penalty case, the jurors are brought in one-by-one and questioned by both the prosecuting attorney and defense counsel.

YOUR RIGHTS: *You have the right to be informed of the date, time, and location of this event and you have the right to be present.*

GUILT PHASE

The guilt phase generally begins with the prosecutor's opening statement. The defense then has the option to make an opening statement or, in some jurisdictions, reserve its opening statement for the beginning of its case-in-chief. The prosecutor presents the state's direct case, after which the defense may move for the court to acquit, arguing that there is legally insufficient evidence to convict.

If the defense motion is denied, the defense presents its case-in-chief. Following the defense case, the prosecutor and defendant may each present a rebuttal case. The defense may then again move for an acquittal. If the defense motion is denied, closing arguments are presented by each side; the order in which they are presented is determined by the rules of the specific jurisdiction. Following closing arguments, the case is submitted to the jury or bench for deliberation and return of a verdict.

YOUR RIGHTS: *You have the right to be informed of the date, time, and location of this event, and you have the right to be present.*

SENTENCING

Upon a finding of guilt on some or all counts charged, the formal imposition of the punishment occurs. Depending upon the jurisdiction, either the judge or the jury decides the punishment that will be given to the offender. In most jurisdictions, before a sentencing hearing is conducted, a probation officer prepares a presentence report. Most reports contain a variety of information that may be helpful in imposing sentence: information about the offender's prior criminal record, personal characteristics, financial condition, social history, and circumstances affecting his or her behavior. In addition, most jurisdictions now require that these reports contain victim information. Generally, a sentencing hearing cannot occur unless the offender is present, although this requirement may be waived in certain instances. In addition, in most jurisdictions the victim has the right to be present and to give a victim impact statement at the sentencing hearing.

At the sentencing hearing, the court generally has three options. First, the court may impose sentence, which may include imprisonment or some other punishment such as probation, community service, or a treatment program. Second, in many jurisdictions the court may decide not to sentence the offender, but instead to suspend imposition of sentence and place the offender on probation. Finally, the court may impose sentence, but suspend execution of it and place the offender on probation subject to conditions. After sentence is imposed, the court enters a judgment of conviction, setting forth the plea, verdict, findings, adjudication, and sentence imposed. At this point, the defense attorney may make a motion to set aside the verdict.

YOUR RIGHTS: *You have the right to be informed of the date, time, and location of this event, and you have the right to be present. You also have the right to give a victim impact statement. (See Arraignment. You should ask for restitution at this time. See below.)*

RESTITUTION

Restitution is the monetary payment by an offender to the victim to compensate the victim for the financial consequences caused by the commission of the crime. Generally, restitution must be requested at or before sentencing. What a victim receives during the criminal case is usually an order for an amount of restitution and a payment schedule. Once an offender is released from prison and is no longer on probation, a victim may have to go to civil court to convert a restitution order into a civil judgment in order to collect additional monies.

YOUR RIGHTS: *You have the right to request restitution in your case if you have experienced financial hardship as a result of the crime. Talk to your victim advocate and prosecutor to establish the appropriate amount to request and to ensure it is requested by the court. This is an area that very often is not followed through on for crime victims, especially if they do not attend the hearing and leave it up to the prosecutor.*

APPELLATE REVIEW BY THE DEFENDANT OR THE STATE

Appellate review is the way you ask a higher court to review what the lower court or a lower actor in the system has done to make sure they did it right. There are a number of avenues for seeking appellate review in a criminal case, but each is specifically set forth in law and some attach only to the defendant or the state, leaving the victim with fewer remedies. The most common appellate review devices are

- *Interlocutory appeal.* This is an appeal of a nonfinal court decision that may occur any time before the final judgment.

- *Direct appeal.* A direct appeal may be taken after the final judgment has been rendered.

- *Postconviction relief.* A postconviction motion may be brought by the defendant.

- *Habeas corpus.* A defendant may petition for habeas corpus under both state and federal law.

- *Writ of mandamus.* A writ of mandamus is an extraordinary writ that compels performance of a mandatory duty.

- *Writ of prohibition.* A writ of prohibition is an extraordinary writ issued by a higher court to a lower court prohibiting that lower court from acting beyond its jurisdiction.

YOUR RIGHTS: *You have the right to be informed of the date, time, and location of this event, you have the right to be present, and you may have the right to be heard depending upon the proceeding.*

PROBATION AND PROBATION REVOCATION HEARINGS

Probation is a procedure under which a defendant found guilty of a crime is not imprisoned but instead is released subject to conditions imposed by the court and subject to the supervision of a board of probation or parole, or the jurisdiction's equivalent. If a defendant is accused of violating the conditions of probation, generally he or she may be arrested and brought to court for a hearing to determine whether there is probable cause to conclude that a violation took place. If probable cause is found, or if the defendant waives the hearing, the defendant is subject to a revocation hearing to have probation revoked and to be resentenced.

YOUR RIGHTS: *You have the right to be informed of the date, time, and location of this event, and you have the right to be present and to be heard prior to a decision.*

PAROLE AND PAROLE REVOCATION HEARINGS

Parole is the release of an offender to the community by the court or a probation or parole board prior to the expiration of the offender's term, subject to conditions imposed by the court or board. In many jurisdictions, offenders are eligible for parole prior to the completion of their entire sentence. Generally, before an offender is released, there is a parole hearing to determine if there is reasonable probability that the offender can be released without detriment to the community. If it is determined that it is proper to release the offender, the offender is released but remains in the legal custody of the department of corrections, or the jurisdiction's equivalent, and is subject to conditions placed on him or her. If the offender violates any of the conditions imposed, generally he or she may be arrested, incarcerated, and, unless it is waived, given a preliminary hearing on whether the alleged violation occurred. Following the preliminary hearing, the offender will generally have a full parole revocation hearing at which there is a determination of whether a violation took place and whether to revoke parole.

YOUR RIGHTS: *You have the right to be informed of the date, time, and location of this event, and you have the right to be present and to be heard prior to a decision.*

COMPENSATION

Compensation, sometimes referred to as reparations, is money paid by the government to victims of crimes to restore all or part of the financial losses the victim suffered as a result of the crime committed against him or her.

YOUR RIGHTS: *As with restitution, you have the right to be financially compensated for things such as medical and counseling expenses, loss of earnings, loss of support, stolen cash, relocation, funeral expenses, or crime scene cleanup. The best way to file a claim is with the help of a victim advocate at your local victim services program. It is important to note the difference between restitution and compensation for victims: restitution is money that the court orders the defendant to pay; compensation is money the government pays for out-of-pocket costs you incur. If the court orders restitution in your case for expenses for which you also filed for compensation, it is important for you to know that the government should be the recipient of the restitution and not you. You cannot be reimbursed twice—if the compensation program pays out a claim to you and then restitution is ordered by the court, the compensation program should then be awarded the restitution. Every state has a compensation program; to find yours, go to http://www.nacvcb.org/.*

This was a long chapter with a lot of information and legal terminology. No doubt you will want to come back to this chapter time and time again while your case proceeds through the criminal justice process. Important things to remember are that you are not alone, and you do not have to digest all this information now. Victim advocates are available who are willing to walk you through each and every step of this process. Just as we have sponsors in our various twelve-step programs who guide us through our recovery, victim advocates can do the same with regard to all the information in this chapter and more. Reach out to them, pick up the phone, and don't do this alone.

EXERCISE

Take a moment to write down any questions that came up for you while reading this chapter so you don't forget to ask them later.

Take a moment to write here or on a separate piece
of paper, or just process out loud or in your mind,
a gratitude list.

What are ten things you are grateful for today?

_____

_____

_____

_____

_____

_____

_____

_____

_____

_____

_____

_____

_____

_____

CHAPTER TEN

To Forgive or Not to Forgive?

Forgiveness is a hot topic in the criminal justice system. It is often referred to as restorative justice, although that is not completely accurate. Restorative justice is a process that engages both the victim and the offender in a manner that empowers them both to take individual active approaches in repairing the harm incurred by the criminal act. The concept is to look at the crime itself not as being against the state or those holding the criminal charges, but as being a crime against the victim or the community, thus placing the impact where it ought to be. Yes, offenders break the law and must be accountable to the state and the courts, but restorative justice allows for the emotional impact of the crime to come to the forefront in the hope of healing for all parties involved.

The victim is empowered to be active in the process by becoming willing to engage the community or offender in a way that would enable the victim to communicate the effect the crime has had on him or her, while the offender is encouraged to take responsibility for his or her actions. This process often results in a type of dialogue between the victim and offender, whether it is during the victim impact statement process, via an apology letter written by the offender, or in a face-to-face meeting between the victim and offender. Many states have created dialogue programs or victim-offender mediation programs that prepare both the offender and the victim to meet to discuss issues surrounding the crime. If your state doesn't have a dialogue program, you can reach out to your local or state victim advocacy program and see if they can facilitate this process for you.

Whether to participate in such a program is a personal decision for you as a victim to make, and it is not one that should be entered into lightly or without consultation with those you trust. If you live in a state with an established program, then you will be ahead of the game, as the advocates in that program will walk you through the process that will potentially bring you and your offender together. You should be clear about what your goals are, what you are expecting to ask, and what expectations you have—or, as in recovery, you do not have. This may seem like a contradiction in terms, so let me explain. We know that having expectations can be a dangerous place for us in our addiction. Expectations can serve as the motivators for engaging in things that could potentially prove to be harmful to our recovery.

Anytime we have an idea in our head about the way a situation may or may not unfold in our lives, we begin to insert our own agenda into that situation, and in many ways we set ourselves up for failure. In recovery, that type of failure can be deadly or extremely detrimental. It could mean that our emotions around the outcome of a situation could send us into a tailspin of anger, hatred, and resentment. These types of emotions can be toxic for our recovery, and often are the very things that lead us directly into engaging in negative behaviors and falling back into our addiction. It is important to not make these decisions about forgiveness lightly; they must come on your terms and in a manner that will further your healing, not hinder it.

When thinking about your goals for engaging an offender, it is important to realize that you have no control over the outcome, and therefore it is best to have limited and very specific expectations or no real expectations of his or her behavior or the outcome. Restorative justice can be similar to when we make amends in a recovery program. We do this for ourselves—we do not do it to get answers; we do not do it to have someone tell us he or she is sorry; we do not do it for any reason other than to clear our side of the street. In the case of your victimization, there may not be any clear responsibility you need to take—after all, crime is something completely outside your control; another's harm of you and your family is beyond your realm of accountability.

As a crime victim you probably have a million questions you want to ask, and a dialogue program may be right for you. I advise against attempting to arrange a dialogue with your offender on your own without someone to assist in mediating the discussion, both prior to the face-to-face meeting and during the meeting. Ask your victim advocate or counselor if your state has an established mediation program; if they do, they will have trained advocates and counselors who can take you through this process. You will need support and someone to ensure that the conversation stays on track and that you are not harmed any further. If your state doesn't already have an established program, you can attempt to do this with your local victim services program and see what your options are.

Engaging a person in a dialogue does not mean that you forgive that person, it just means you have questions and are open to seeking answers. That dialogue could lead to your own personal forgiveness, or it could result in forgiving the offender—but that isn't always the case.

Be very careful if your case is high-profile in nature, as media outlets and programs may try to get you to have this dialogue on TV. I have spoken with many crime victims whose cases were high-profile, and they were actively sought out to engage in discussions with their offenders on camera. This is your choice, and only you know what is right for you. Just recognize that if you choose to go this route, there are things you need to know that producers, reporters, and other media personnel may not share with you. The first one is that in most cases the offender will be paid for the interview—in fact, this is how most media outlets get offenders to participate in something public. This should be a factor for you because it could mean the motivation of your offender is not sincere and may be financially motivated. Whatever you decide, ensure that your recovery is on the right track, as you wouldn't want to engage in anything that could lead you to a relapse.

I spoke again with Debra Puglisi Sharp about her understanding and experiences with self-forgiveness and the role that addiction played in her life as a result of her victimization. Here is what she had to say:

Self-forgiveness: In April of 1998 my husband of twenty-five years was murdered. I was then raped in our home, kidnapped, and held hostage at my rapist's home for five days before I escaped. Intense psychotherapy ensued within one month of the crime, and I was diagnosed with post-traumatic stress disorder. The past twelve and a half years have been a journey of healing for me and my adult children. Taking a Xanax in the morning seemed to keep my anxiety in check until five o'clock in the evening. There were times when I could rationalize having a glass of wine in the afternoon—after all, it was "five o'clock somewhere." Medicating with alcohol had become a crutch for me. Just recently I returned to psychotherapy. I had only recently admitted that I have addiction when I finally realized that this unhealthy habit of mine must be addressed. I now discuss the painful issues that I have been avoiding with alcohol, as well as the guilt I have carried over the years, openly with my counselor. As I learned many years ago, part of the healing process is forgiving yourself. Recently I looked at myself in the mirror and saw a woman in pain. The first step was to admit I had this problem. The second step was to call and make that first appointment to return to counseling. It is not easy to admit my imperfections. Being a co-owner of two taverns, I see the same people drinking every day. I guess they are hurting in some way too. I had to hit rock bottom before reality kicked in, landing me in the emergency room with severe heartburn and other symptoms that had to be ruled out as indicating a heart attack. Once I was told that I did not have heart disease, I had to come to grips with the fact that all of the alcohol I had been consuming was eroding my esophagus. Thank goodness I did not develop an ulcer.

I have since forgiven myself for indulging during these past years since my victimization, realizing that recovery does not happen overnight. It helps to have a loving, supportive husband who does not judge me. My goal is to continue therapy and become well again. In the meantime, I will not allow guilt to hinder my progress. I am living one day at a time and taking better care of myself.

As Debra so eloquently stated, everyone's process is different. Forgiveness is a choice, not a requirement of the process of healing after victimization. You may never choose to forgive your offender, and that is okay—as long as you are not holding on to anger, resentment, shame, or other harmful emotions as a result of not forgiving. Anger, resentment, and shame are the toxic emotions that can lead us directly into our addictive behaviors again. It is vital that we stay in tune with our emotional state and ensure we are not masking our feelings.

It also is important to identify whether or not you are withholding forgiveness as a means of holding on to these toxic emotions, or if you are at peace with what happened and are choosing not to forgive. For many people forgiveness can be tied up in control, and this can be a struggle. Anger, resentment, hatred, and shame may have been your motivators for so long that the thought of releasing these emotions could feel like losing control. They may have been what's gotten you out of bed each day or given you the strength to stand up in court and testify. The thought of letting go of these emotions by forgiving could be a terrifying concept.

EXERCISE

Grab your notebook or journal and take a moment to think about forgiveness. Try to define it for yourself. What would forgiving your offender look like to you? What would this forgiveness mean to you? What feelings come up for you when you think about this? What would forgiveness do to those feelings and emotions? Can you live without those feelings? Can you forgive?

Forgiveness may mean involving your offender in some way, such as through the processes listed at the beginning of this chapter. This concept of restorative justice is something that Debra has some opinions on as well:

> Restorative justice. This controversial subject has raised serious questions for me. Why do so many people ask me if I have forgiven my offender? I do not mind answering the question when I speak publicly, as the audience consists of law enforcement personnel, health professionals, victim service providers, and others who truly care about assisting victims. These particular groups have never pressured me into believing that forgiveness is essential in order to recover. On the other hand, I do get the feeling that society feels it takes courage to forgive, and perhaps I would find peace and healing by forgiving the man who killed my husband, kidnapped me, and raped me repeatedly while he held me hostage. None of these people have walked in my shoes. Having received the US Attorney General's Special Courage Award in Washington, DC, on the nine-year anniversary of my crime in 2007 validated my courage. I am happily remarried and am passionate about my work in the community to assist victims of crime.
>
> It was brought to my attention that some victim advocates actually place "forgive the offender" on their list of things to do for their victim to heal. Forgiveness is a personal choice. You cannot "fix" victims by encouraging them to forgive, thereby achieving recovery. I have talked to victims who have made that choice to forgive, and I fully respect their decision. Some have found that they are unable to lead a normal life until forgiveness is granted. I compare forgiveness to the grieving process. As a hospice nurse, I constantly remind families that everyone grieves differently. The same applies to forgiveness. It is right for some and not for others.

During my travels across the United States over the past ten years, I have been approached by hundreds of victims who remain in pain. Some have told me that they feel bad because they cannot bring themselves to forgive their offender. Society has placed this burden upon them. Personally, I believe in God and feel that He may forgive the man who murdered my husband. It is not my job. In many ways, I have become an advocate for victims who feel as I do. I listen and let them know that I respect whatever decision they make.

No one should judge a victim for deciding not to forgive. I hear comments such as "I hope he burns in hell," or "He deserves the same punishment." These victims are obviously in a huge amount of pain. Who am I to say, "You must forgive so that you can move on"? I listen and offer support. A victim should not be told how to feel.

When an offender sets out to purposely harm another person, the act of forgiveness becomes more difficult. Every crime is different. If my husband had been struck and killed by a drunk driver, I think forgiving his murderer would be much easier. Driving under the influence of alcohol is no good excuse; however, the intention of murder was not present. My offender confessed to his crime, telling law enforcement that he set out to kidnap and rape a woman. My husband got in his way, so he shot him and persisted until he got what he wanted—me. While holding me hostage and raping me, he told me that his profession was "crime" and that he believed he had committed the perfect crime. I cannot begin to explain the terror I felt as he sodomized me. He was actually joyful when I screamed in pain. If I had not escaped, I am convinced he would have killed me. That is what I live with.

What person can explain to me that I should forgive my offender? A judge and jury placed him behind bars for the rest of his life. If he were released, I have no doubt this person would rape again, and if anyone tried to get in his way he would have no problem killing that person.

Forgiveness should be an option. I still have not closed the door. A friend of mine is the founder of Victims' Voices Heard in Delaware. We have had many conversations, and in fact, when the time is right, I plan to begin the restorative justice process with her assistance. Before I begin the process, I must be certain that I am physically and mentally capable of facing my offender. Of course, he must agree to the meeting. My fear is that he will not grant permission. There is so much I want to say to this man who changed my life forever. My relationship with my children has been altered because of the ongoing grief and differences of opinion when it comes to my work in victim advocacy. I am not the same person. How could I be? It has been difficult for Melissa and Michael to see their mother on national television, discussing the gruesome details of a horrific crime. Damn Donald Flagg. He stole my children's dreams of the family they remember. Does a man who confesses to being a criminal deserve forgiveness? Meeting with my husband's murderer may or may not result in my decision to forgive. The ball will be in his court. If he is truly remorseful, perhaps I will say the words "I forgive you." That does not mean that I will ever forget.

I plan to leave the door open. My rewards come by giving back to a community that has supported me. I serve on many committees and have vowed to empower victims to become survivors. When the time is right to reconsider forgiveness, I will know it. In the meantime, God will not judge me for taking the time to figure this all out. Who knows? I may just leave it up to Him.

Debra's experience only highlights again that everyone's process is their own, and that there is no right or wrong answer when it comes to forgiving your offender or offenders.

Personal forgiveness—that is, forgiving yourself—is very different and is an important part of the recovery process. Forgiving yourself for whatever perceived faults you may have in relation to your victimization is crucial to your healing. Carrying around those toxic emotions we have been talking about is dangerous for our recovery and can make us a ticking time bomb for relapse. Remember, our best tool in recovery is self-awareness. The more on top of our emotional well-being we are on any given day, the more prepared we are to recognize addictive thinking when it returns and addictive behaviors when we begin to engage in them. We are not perfect people, and these things will happen. As long as we have a solid grasp of who we are and how we feel, we should be able to identify potentially dangerous thinking and behaviors before they cause us to relapse.

EXERCISE

Grab your notebook or journal and consider the following questions:

Do I need to forgive myself?

Am I holding on to toxic emotions regarding this crime that are leading me to blame myself in some way?

What would it mean to forgive myself?

What feelings come up when I think about forgiving myself?

What would personal forgiveness feel like or look like in my life?

Forgiveness can be both a gateway to emotional freedom and a floodgate of emotional release that we weren't prepared for. As always, be gentle with yourself. You do not have to find forgiveness today or tomorrow. It is important to identify whether or not the lack of forgiveness will lead to a relapse for you, and I hope that through reading about Debra's journey and doing the exercises in this chapter, you have a better feel for where you are in this process. Remember, it's about progress, not perfection.

Take a moment to write here or on a separate piece
of paper, or just process out loud or in your mind,
a gratitude list.

What are eleven things you are grateful for today?

_____

_____

_____

_____

_____

_____

_____

_____

_____

_____

_____

_____

CHAPTER ELEVEN

Closure

*"People kept telling me that I had to find closure,
but I had no idea where to look."*

*"After my son was murdered, nothing could bring me closure. This
crime was an open wound that I knew I would have for life. I just
had to figure out a way to heal it each and every day."*

"We will not regret the past nor wish to shut the door on it" is
something we hear all the time in the promises of recovery. Our
past makes up who we are today, and in recovery we learn to
appreciate all the bumps in the road that got us to where we are.
In recovery, we have no doubt taken countless walks down the path of
our history; we have unearthed the decisions, events, and experiences
that have shaped us and that led to our addictive behaviors and
eventually to our recovery. Once you have done the footwork required
in recovery, you may feel that you have closure on that aspect of
your life. Now you are faced with a new path, with a new round of
experiences and feelings surrounding an event, and this may make it
feel like closure is not an option.

But can you move on without closure? Is it possible to find closure after such a devastating event? Does closure come when the person is arrested? At the trial? When the offender is convicted or sentenced? What if your offender is never apprehended, or what if he or she is found not-guilty? Trying to find closure is a long and very personal process to undertake when you are victimized by crime. It is important to find methods that work for you, rather than what others want or need from you. It is also critical that you accept that there may never be closure. For those who have experienced violent crime, such as rape or homicide, closure is most likely an elusive concept.

Although closure may be something that isn't possible, I don't want you to discount it. You may find that you can reach this place and move forward. Just know that it is not a requirement for healing. Some people equate closure with peace, with a crossing over from pain to recovery. Some feel that once the case has gone through the entire judicial system and sentencing has occurred and they have spoken, they have closure. That is perfectly fine if that is where you are. That is a wonderful thing for you, and you should honor that.

For some of you, there may never be a criminal justice process to walk through. While I was able to outline much of the system as you may experience it, I haven't yet touched on the factors that could come into play that would take the criminal justice system and your participation in it completely out of the picture—possibly making this concept of closure even more elusive to you. The following are some barriers you may face in terms of finding closure:

YOUR OFFENDER WAS NEVER FOUND

Though in most criminal cases a person is arrested and charged, there are many cases that go unsolved for years, for decades, or even forever. Then victims are faced with the horrors of wondering on a minute-to-minute basis where their offender is and if they are safe from him or her, whether he or she will ever be brought to justice, and what it means if he or she is not. How do you obtain justice if your offender isn't found? How do you live each and every day knowing the person is still out there and could strike again? In this case you must find a way to go on. Focusing on ensuring your safety is of utmost priority. Work with your close support system, your victim advocate, and anyone else you trust to ensure you and your loved ones are safe from harm. This may mean that you have to make some hard decisions, such as moving away to a place that is unknown. Whatever you need to do to feel free and safe again is vital for your healing and recovery. If you put into place a strategy that enables you to feel comfortable and safe, you may be able to find peace and serenity again.

YOU NEVER REPORTED THE CRIME OR DO NOT WISH TO PURSUE CHARGES

Crimes go unreported for a host of reasons. The most common unreported crimes are rape, sexual assault, and domestic violence. Often the shame, guilt, fear, and anxiety that go into reporting these types of crimes outweigh the need or desire for justice. Maybe you or someone else did call the police initially, but after processing all the factors you have decided not to move forward with charges. No one can make you report a crime of this nature, as it is such a personal attack on you. However, please note that sometimes if there is sufficient evidence to charge a suspect, it may not be your decision. More often prosecutors and police are moving forward with these types of charges without the cooperation of the victim. It is important for you to know that your participation in the criminal justice system may not be voluntary, and to understand that you may be subpoenaed to court against your will and be required to testify. If you do not testify or if you lie under oath, you could face charges yourself. There are many skilled attorneys and victim advocates who will do everything in their power to protect you from this; however, if it happens you will be faced with a decision. If we live by the principles of our recovery, then lying isn't an option.

YOUR OFFENDER WAS FOUND NOT GUILTY

I have seen more cases than I care to recall that have gone through the criminal justice system and a jury has rendered a not-guilty verdict. This can be the biggest blow and revictimization for a person. It can stir up all the feelings discussed in this book and more when it comes to your healing process. As hard as it is, you have to find a way to separate yourself from the conclusion of this process, as it is so far out of your control. So many factors go into a criminal case: the prosecution; the judge and any rulings he or she makes during the course of the case; the defense tactics; the testimony of various parties who may or may not tell the truth, the whole truth, and nothing but the truth. And then there is the wildest wild card of them all—the jury.

Imagine gathering up twelve of your friends or family members and trying to get them all to decide on one conclusion. When was the last time you tried to get your family or friends to decide upon dinner or a movie? It is not an easy task to get that many people to agree on something simple, so put yourself in the shoes of a juror, or twelve jurors having to look at everything they are presented with and come to a unanimous, or at least majority, decision that will change the lives of many people forever. In some cases it could mean someone's freedom, in others, perhaps someone's life. This is a challenging process for jurors.

Jurors are everyday people just like you and me, and even though they are instructed not to, it is difficult for them to not bring their own prejudices, feelings, and experiences into the decision-making process. Additionally, jurors don't always get the entire picture. Because of the way our system is structured, sometimes important details, such as prior convictions, are eliminated from a case by way of legal motions. This can be infuriating to the victim because the inclusion of this information might lead the jury to a different conclusion.

The conclusion of your criminal or civil trial is so far out of your hands that to invest too much in its outcome can lead to very damaging emotional results. You know what happened, and you know your own truth. Find a way to honor your truth and be at peace with whatever outcome may occur so that you can move forward.

YOUR OFFENDER WAS KILLED OR HAS SINCE DIED

It is possible that your offender was killed in the commission of the crime or as a result of his or her apprehension. Or your offender may have died elsewhere as a result of natural causes or another crime, perhaps. Your offender could die in prison awaiting trial or sentencing. These scenarios can bring up all kinds of mixed emotions, and if this is the case for you, it is important that you give each of those emotions due respect as part of your healing process. You may feel great relief and joy at the news of your offender's death. You may feel a sudden pang of sadness and/or grief. You may also feel absolutely nothing at this news. Whatever you feel, work through it and process those feelings or the lack of feelings to the best of your ability either with your counselor, in your support groups, or with your higher power, sponsor, or another trusted source.

Your offender's death could bring an end to a process that you felt you needed to engage in to find answers. Now you must find a way to seek those answers on your own and come to some sort of conclusion that you can live with. You may never know all the answers, and you may have to find a way to be okay and to move forward with the information that you do have.

If you have found closure in some part of the process and feel completely at peace, good for you! If you feel that you will never have closure, you will have to come to terms with the fact that it is okay not to have closure. For those of you who believe closure is not a concept in your reality anymore, you are now finding ways to tend to those open wounds. You are walking through life with an understanding that this event has had an impact on you that could last forever, and there is no end point. Find whatever works for you and work it.

EXERCISE

What do you need in order to walk through life in spite of this event?

What answers would help you to move on?

Do you believe in closure, and if so, what does that look like for you?

Can you move forward in your life without it?

Take a moment to write here or on a separate piece
of paper, or just process out loud or in your mind,
a gratitude list.

What are twelve things you are grateful for today?

_____

_____

_____

_____

_____

_____

_____

_____

_____

_____

_____

_____

CHAPTER TWELVE

A New Normal

Crime victims often ask me what it will take for them to feel normal again. The word "normal" can become a trap, because once crime affects your life, things are never truly the same. The crime and all the events surrounding it are now woven into the very fabric of who you are, and you have been changed by this experience. You will most likely never feel exactly the way you did before the crime. This isn't to insinuate that you aren't "okay" or "normal" by a textbook definition; after all, what does "normal" mean, and who gets to define what is and what isn't normal? By virtue of your victimization, the definition of what is normal for you now has to change. In the victim services community we call this a "new normal." This should not be viewed as a bad thing; however, it is *different.*

In your recovering life you are different from the person you were in your active addiction, right? The same goes for this new experience. The healthiest way to cope with this new normal is to understand and accept it as what your life is today, and to try not to dwell on what you used to be like and what you are missing. Your life may have been turned completely inside out and upside down, and while working through this book is helping you begin to get things in order, you still have a long road ahead of you. This is a lifelong process and a daily practice, just like recovery.

I hope that throughout this book you were able to walk through your feelings surrounding the crime, one feeling in particular being grief. Another area where you may experience grief is over the loss of your previous "normal" life. In recovery, when we finally make the decision to accept that we are addicted and we make a commitment to recovery, we go through a grief process. That process is the grieving for our old lives or old self. Our addiction ruled our lives, and when we begin to change—albeit most of the time for the better—it is an extreme event and we feel the void or loss of it.

When you go through an extreme trauma, you are likely to feel a similar void. There may be things you can no longer do as a result of the victimization, whether as a result of physical or emotional injury. There may be places you can no longer go because they are too painful or hold significant reminders of the victimization. There may be people you can no longer see as a result of the crime. All of these things create voids within us, and a void left unattended can become a pitfall in our recovery and healing. We want to be sure to tend to these voids in a healthy manner to avoid returning to addictive behaviors.

EXERCISE

Grab your notebook and take a moment to think about what is different in your life now. Are there places you can no longer go? People you can no longer see? Smells you can no longer tolerate? Foods you cannot eat? List all the things you have lost as a result of this victimization, and then answer this question: how does the loss of these things change your "normal" everyday life?

You may also have gained a lot through this process. Bad actions can sometimes have positive reactions in our lives. It is okay to acknowledge that through this painful experience you may have gained something. It doesn't invalidate in any way the horrible experience you have faced. This may seem like an odd concept to accept at first, but as part of our healing it is okay for us to identify personal growth as a result of unexpected and involuntary events that happen in our lives. These changes are also now a part of your new normal, and it is important to be aware of them. An example from my victimization would be that I never knew victims' rights existed, let alone what they were and how to access them. Today I am a strong advocate for victims' rights, I work on legislation, and I run a nonprofit organization that helps other victims. It is important to be able to look at the positive side of who we are today.

For some people, one victimization might lead to the processing and healing of a past victimization or trauma that they didn't realize they had to work through until faced with the new trauma.

EXERCISE

Try to think of things you have gained as a result of this crime. What have you learned? How do the things you have gained change your "normal" everyday life?

So what is your new normal? Who are you now that you have been through this experience?

When something traumatic happens, many of us tend to analyze everything. We look at every angle of our lives to see how things are now, and how they might have been had X happened or Y not happened. Our new normal may also lead us to look at the world and our role in it differently. We realize that our time isn't infinite, and that all the things we are putting off to do until tomorrow now, in a sense, have an expiration date.

EXERCISE

In your notebook or journal, write a "bucket list"—a list of all the things you want to accomplish in life before you die. Be as truthful as you possibly can, not thinking about the potential logistical obstacles, but simply listing all the things you would like to do.

It is so important for us to have things to look forward to. Life goes on regardless of what we go through, and what we do with our time here matters. You have overcome so much. You have battled your demons; you have actively pursued a healthier life by committing every day to not engaging in addictive behavior, and to getting up the next day and starting over; and now you have survived a horrible trauma. You deserve some good in your life. You deserve some rewards. Set your bucket list in a prominent location in your life, whether it is on your bedroom mirror, bathroom mirror, or kitchen refrigerator—someplace you will see it every day. Let it serve as a vivid reminder of the dreams you have, and start taking the steps needed to be able to cross off the items on your list. If there is anything you should believe in today, it is that you can overcome anything, and you can do anything you set your mind to. You are a survivor.

Take a moment to write here or on a separate piece
of paper, or just process out loud or in your mind,
a gratitude list.

What are thirteen things you are grateful for today?

_____

_____

_____

_____

_____

_____

_____

_____

_____

_____

_____

_____

_____

CHAPTER THIRTEEN

Survive and Thrive

"I thought I would always feel like a victim, like someone else had control over a part of me. I no longer identify myself as a victim; today, I am a survivor."

Your victimization does not have to define who you are, but it can certainly serve as a motivation for you to want to make change. Just as many of us have overcome extreme adversity in our addiction, we can overcome our victimization and learn to live healthy, happy, and free again. You do not have to remain a victim forever; through this process and the hard work you have done, you are a survivor, and that is something that you should feel very proud of. For many of you this is the end of the road. You have done the footwork, and you have found a place of peace inside you and with the crime. Now it is time to move forward and continue on your path as the new person you are, and I am so happy to have been along with you for some of your journey. I do truly hope the words and exercises in this book have worked for you in a way that has enabled you to find peace, serenity, and growth in your life and recovery.

For some of you this is only the beginning of a whole new journey that may include a life of advocacy and activism. Going through an experience like this has changed you in ways you never could have imagined. As you have gone through each chapter of this book and each phase of your process, you have grown, and you have educated yourself, and some of you may be thinking, *Now what? I want to do something with all this new energy I have.*

When I first found recovery, I was so enthralled by the changes in my life and the hope I finally felt that I wanted nothing more than to help others. I wanted to translate the knowledge and the feelings that I had to others who I knew needed it. There is a saying in recovery: "You only keep what you have by giving it away." Indeed, if you follow a twelve-step program, then you understand this as the Twelfth Step, which teaches us about carrying the message to others. There are many ways you can use your experience to carry the message to others. I went to college to become a drug and alcohol counselor, and while in college I became a victim of a crime, which thrust me into the same process you are in now. After not getting the right services and treatment by the criminal justice system, I had to find out what victims' rights were on my own, and that led me into the work that I do now.

"I knew on a cellular level
that I had to take all that I had
experienced and learned and use
that knowledge to help others."

If you are feeling the same way, that is wonderful. There are many ways to make changes in this broken world, and I hope I can give you many ideas for how you can get involved and help others.

Legislate

Many survivors get involved in legislation and activism. Maybe the crime that affected you could have been prevented as a result of a new law or other change that needs to occur. Maybe your loved one was harmed or killed due to negligence of the system. There are so many gaps and holes in our various systems, so if you can effect change and help to prevent another crime from happening, then that is a beautiful thing. Your voice and experience are what is needed to push this type of change forward. Legislators and policymakers need to hear from those who are affected by the cracks in the system; they need to put a face on a piece of legislation in order to fully understand its impact. Maybe your face, your strength, and your story can be the catalyst to create positive change.

So many people think they cannot get involved in legislation—that it is complicated and so unknown. So is everything in life that you've never done before. The best way to start is to meet with your local representatives and senators. Share your story and ideas with them or their staff if you cannot get a face-to-face meeting right away. Talk to your local victims' advocacy groups and see if they are currently working on any legislation that you could be of assistance with, and you will be doing this work in no time. The victims' rights movement can always use more voices, more feet on the ground, and more supporters in the fight to prevent crime and ensure that crime victims are never going through their trauma alone.

If you have been in recovery for any period of time, you have heard all about the importance of service work. It is a great way for people in early recovery and beyond to get out of themselves and be of help to others. It makes us accountable for something, gives us a commitment to another person or group, and ultimately provides us with a bit of purpose—especially at a time when finding purpose can be so hard. In the time after your victimization, you may find that the simple act of being of service to someone else or something else makes you feel better. Service comes in many forms and does not have to be a major commitment on your part. It can be working the hotline one night a week for a local rape crisis or domestic violence center, collecting items for a local charity, participating in a charitable event, volunteering to provide rides to local support groups, to people in need, or watching children on court days at the courthouse. Whatever type of work that will help you feel like you are giving back and making a difference is the best type of service to find.

Volunteer

If legislation isn't your thing, you can volunteer with an organization to help others. Every nonprofit organization needs volunteers, and there are so many worthy activities you can engage in to help other crime victims. Many organizations have volunteer training programs that give you much of the training to provide services to crime victims such as going to court with victims, providing hotline assistance, and even doing some supportive counseling. This is a wonderful way to give back, because survivors are able to relate to other survivors in a powerful way. Think about twelve-step programs—the core concept is one addict/alcoholic talking to another, in order to learn from those who have been where the newcomer is and who can demonstrate how to move forward in a healthy way. For crime victims, having other survivors come in and support them through their difficult time provides them with the comfort of knowing that not only are they not alone, but they, too, will survive and move forward.

If direct service work isn't your thing, there are other ways you can help nonprofits. I don't know of a nonprofit that doesn't need money, so any assistance you can provide in this area will be of great service. If you are a skilled writer, you can offer your services as a grant writer. Maybe you have always had a flair for event planning. Nonprofits can always use help in planning fundraising events. Whatever talents you have and ways you can give back, they will be appreciated. Just reach out to your local nonprofit organization and let them know that you are there to help. If you don't have much free time, then start slowly by volunteering your time for one specific event, such as a walk or vigil.

Speak

If you are like me, then you have found a new voice as a result of this process, and sharing your story with others can make a great impact. In fact, many states and counties have programs aimed specifically at bringing in crime victims to share their stories with others. Many organizations have speakers' bureaus, and they can be a great place to start your journey as a speaker.

For some, public speaking comes naturally, but for most, public speaking can be hands-down the scariest thing in the world. It is a skill that can be taught, and some speakers' bureaus will provide training to help you tailor your thoughts in a way that is most effective. There is nothing like hearing someone tell his or her story to move others into action or to change thought or behavior patterns. We can never underestimate the power of the spoken word and its effect on us.

There are programs that focus on offenders by using victim impact panels, made up of groups of crime victims who are ready and able to share their experiences with offenders who have either come close to committing a similar crime or who are identified as being high-risk offenders. These programs are proven effective in helping offenders see the potential impact of the crimes they will commit should they stay on the same track that they are on.

Good examples of victim impact panels are those created by Mothers Against Drunk Driving for offenders who are convicted of drunk driving. They bring in survivors of DUIs and families and loved ones who have lost someone to a DUI crash to share their stories with offenders, with the hope that they will see the potential harm they could have caused. These panels have been proven to be successful at decreasing drunk driving. Prisons have similar programs. Many organizations need speakers at vigils, rallies, walks, fundraisers, and the like. Contact your local nonprofit organizations or victims' rights group to learn more about the opportunities available.

Write

As the author of three books, I often have survivors ask me how they, too, can share their experiences in written form. There are many ways you can write and create change. One is to educate yourself about the issues relevant to your experience and write a "letter to the editor" sharing your opinions. A letter to the editor is usually a 250-to-500-word piece that concisely captures your views and is sent to a publication such as a local newspaper or magazine. If you have more to say, you can also look into writing an opinion letter, often referred to as an op-ed. These are usually longer and more in-depth. They typically run about 1,000 to 1,200 words. You can write a letter to the editor or an op-ed to any newspaper in the world—just go online and look up their submission guidelines and go for it!

If you want to write a book, the best advice I can offer is to just do it. Have an idea of what you want to convey with your book, and just start writing. Start writing, and the rest will come. For now, don't worry about editing or flow or chapter structure—those things can be addressed at a later date with revisions or with the help of a talented editor—just write and write and write.

Memoirs and true crime are among some of the best-selling genres of books. People love to read other people's stories of survival of the unthinkable. And just as the writing process may be healing for you, reading your story may be healing for others. Your words and experiences might help get another person through a difficult time. That is why I became a writer, because I knew I had a story to share, and there weren't any books out there like mine yet.

Once you have some pages under your belt and a good sense of what the overall shape of the book will be, then you can start reaching out to literary agents or publishers to determine if what you have is worthy of being published. There are many books and websites that can help you with your writing and with navigating the publishing industry. Google was my main teacher when it came to learning how to write and publish my first book.

Don't let anyone tell you that you cannot become a writer, because you can. If publishing your story isn't your intent, then write it all down for your own personal healing, or to leave for your family history. Another way you can share your thoughts and use writing to create change is to start a blog or a web page.

Create

Art is a powerful medium to educate others, and there are many creative ways in which we can honor ourselves, our process, and our loved ones. For example, the AIDS quilt is a traveling storytelling device that not only shares the lives of those lost to the horrible disease but creates a place for dialogue and educational opportunities wherever it goes. Think outside the box in terms of how you wish to channel your creative energy.

In the final stage of most grief or healing processes, it is natural to want to find some way to memorialize your experience. People do this in all kinds of ways; some engage in the activities stated previously, while others choose more private and personal ways. Debra Puglisi Sharp goes away to a beautiful and serene location each year on the anniversary of her victimization. It is her way of honoring herself during a time she knows will be emotionally hard. Some people do something as simple as lighting a candle and reflecting. Whatever you choose to do with this newfound experience, the one thing that is certain is that you are a survivor, and how you choose to honor that is up to you.

You should be proud of yourself for coming to the end of this book. The exercises in this book may have been hard, and you may have skipped many of them. That is okay. When you are ready, go back to them. As I stated earlier, recovery from anything is all about progress, not perfection. Keep putting one foot in front of the other, and you will be okay. Continue to put your recovery at the forefront of your life. The good, the bad, and the downright ugly days are what make up this journey of life we are all on together. Suit up and show up for your life, because each and every day is a gift.

If we continue to live in gratitude and focus on the positives in our lives, we will always be looking at life in the right way. The majority of our experience in life is how we choose to react to a situation. If we are always focusing on the positive and bringing forth an attitude of gratitude, then we are off to a great start. Thank you for allowing me to assist you in this process in your life. It has been a humbling journey, and I do hope this book has helped you in some way.

Good luck in your adventures.

Resources

To find a victim service provider in your area visit this webpage:
www.ovc.ncjrs.gov/findvictimservices

National Center for Victims of Crime
2000 M Street NW, Suite 480
Washington, DC 20036
phone: 202-467-8700
fax: 202-467-8701
www.ncvc.org

Rape, Abuse & Incest National Network (RAINN)
2000 L Street, NW
Suite 406
Washington, DC 20036
phone: 202-544-3064
fax: 202-544-3556
info@rainn.org
www.rainn.org

The National Sexual Assault Online Hotline is a free, confidential, secure service that provides live help over the RAINN website:
http://apps.rainn.org/ohl-bridge/

Promoting Awareness, Victim Empowerment (PAVE)
PO Box 26354
Alexandria, VA 22313
phone: 877-399-1346
info@pavingtheway.net
www.pavingtheway.net

National Organization for Victim Assistance (NOVA)
510 King Street, Suite 424,
Alexandria, VA 22314
www.trynova.org

National Crime Victim Law Institute (NCVLI)
10015 S.W. Terwilliger Boulevard
Portland, Oregon 97219
phone: 503-768-6600
ncvli@lclark.edu
www.ncvli.org

INTERNATIONAL CRIME VICTIM SERVICES

Before going on your next vacation or business trip outside the United States, make sure to educate yourself about these services. You never know when you will become a victim of crime, and the best defense is an informed offense. So educate yourself and empower yourself. When in another country there may be language barriers you will have to overcome, and services will not always be readily offered to you; you will have to be your own advocate. Ensure that you at least know whom to call if you become a victim.

If you were a victim of a crime while on vacation or traveling in another country, you may have rights you can access. The Office for Victims of Crime has a webpage that allows you to search the rights and services you are afforded.

Please visit the following website to find out what rights or services you are legally entitled to:

http://ovc.ncjrs.gov/findvictimservices/search.asp

Additionally, here are some publications and resources to educate you as to what rights and services you have and where to access them:

http://www.ovc.gov/publications/infores/global.htm.

http://www.amnestyusa.org/international_justice/pdf/IJA_ Factsheet_4_Victims_Rights.pdf

http://www.vaonline.org/advocacy.html

SUBSTANCE ABUSE HELP
If you think you may have a drinking or drug problem

This is a very common thought, and maybe you do and maybe you don't. It isn't my job, or anyone else's for that matter, to tell you whether or not you are an alcoholic or an addict. You must decide that on your own. If you are asking the question, then there must have been some things that have led you to this place. This admission is a very personal one, and the road to recovery is yours and yours alone. But here is the best part...you don't have to travel it alone. There are many resources at your fingertips. Here are but a few of them:

Alcoholics Anonymous (AA)
www.aa.org

Check out the section "Is AA for you?"—it may answer many of your questions.

Narcotics Anonymous (NA)
www.na.org

Check the yellow pages of your phone book for local phone numbers for AA and NA. People are there waiting to listen to you, to help you, and even to take you to a meeting.

www.intherooms.com
InTheRooms is the premier, most comprehensive online social network for the Alcoholics Anonymous and Narcotics Anonymous community worldwide. They are the Facebook for recovering folks, and you can find me on there almost daily. The have resources, articles, speaker tapes, online meetings, rehabilitation directories, and more.

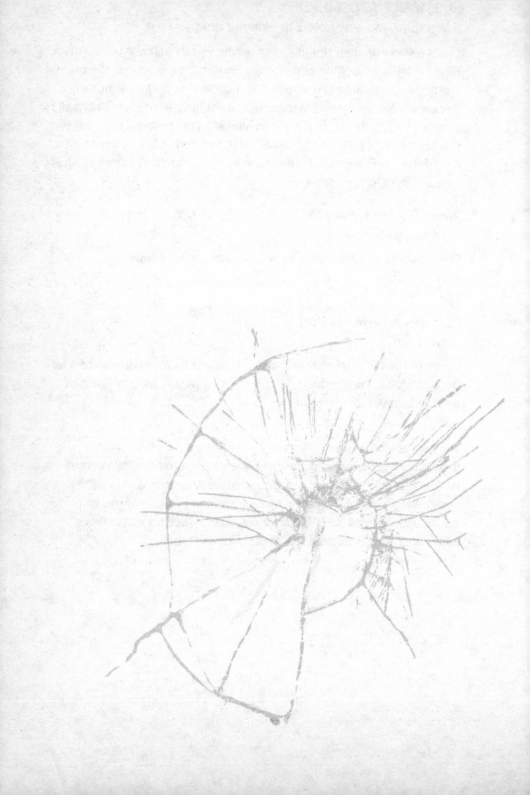